Luis Larraín

The Face of Chile's LGBTQ Movement – Unfiltered

Riko Mendoza

ISBN: 9781779696823
Imprint: Telephasic Workshop
Copyright © 2024 Riko Mendoza.
All Rights Reserved.

Contents

Introduction: Who the Fuck Is Luis Larraín?

Chile's LGBTQ Leader: How Luis Larraín Became the Fucking Voice of Chile's Queer Community

Breaking Fucking Barriers: Larraín's Fucking Journey from Political Activism to Leading LGBTQ Rights in Chile

In this section, we explore the remarkable journey of Luis Larraín, who emerged as a prominent LGBTQ rights advocate in Chile. We delve into the challenges he faced, the milestones he achieved, and the lasting impact he made on the queer community in Chile.

1.1.1 The Fucking Early Years: From Political Activism to LGBTQ Leadership

Luis Larraín, born and raised in Chile during the politically conservative era, experienced the struggles of growing up in an environment that restricted LGBTQ rights and marginalized queer voices. Coming to terms with his own sexuality in a society that criminalized homosexuality was no easy feat. However, it was this personal struggle that fueled his passion for activism and marked the beginning of his journey towards becoming an influential LGBTQ leader.

Larraín realized that true change could only come through political activism. He recognized that it was the conservative political system that perpetuated discrimination and oppression against the LGBTQ community. With an unwavering determination to challenge societal norms and fight for queer rights, Larraín embarked on a mission to break fucking barriers and pave the way for LGBTQ equality.

1.1.2 The Fucking Role of Political Activism: Amplifying LGBTQ Voices

Larraín understood the power of political activism in bringing about systemic change. He recognized that by being actively involved in the political landscape, he could not only make a direct impact on policies and legislation but also raise awareness and amplify the voices of the LGBTQ community. Through his activism, Larraín aimed to challenge the status quo and advocate for equality and justice.

One of the key aspects of Larraín's political activism was his ability to build alliances with like-minded individuals and LGBTQ rights organizations. By uniting different groups with a shared vision, he could mobilize a more significant force for change. Through community organizing, Larraín established networks that provided support, resources, and advocacy opportunities for LGBTQ individuals.

1.1.3 The Fucking Importance of Representation: Shaping LGBTQ Identities

Larraín recognized the profound impact of representation in shaping public opinion and challenging societal biases. In a society where LGBTQ individuals were often stigmatized and excluded, he sought to create visibility and acceptance through various media platforms and public speaking engagements.

By sharing his own personal experiences as an openly gay man, Larraín aimed to humanize the LGBTQ community and break down stereotypes. His courageous storytelling inspired countless individuals struggling with their sexual identity to embrace their true selves. Through representation, Larraín empowered others to embrace their sexuality and fight for their rights.

1.1.4 Overcoming Fucking Conservative Resistance: Navigating the Political Landscape

Larraín encountered numerous obstacles and faced several challenges while navigating Chile's conservative political system. He confronted opposition from conservative politicians and religious leaders who systematically perpetuated homophobia and discrimination. Larraín's ability to navigate these obstacles while staying true to his cause showcased his resilience and determination.

Through strategic alliances and a relentless pursuit of justice, Larraín sought to change public perception and confront systemic homophobia head-on. He engaged in public debates, challenged discriminatory policies, and utilized the power of media to hold those in power accountable. This unwavering resolve to push against conservative resistance became a defining characteristic of Larraín's journey.

1.1.5 The Fucking Future of LGBTQ Activism in Chile: Carrying Larraín's Fucking Legacy Forward

Luis Larraín's journey from political activism to becoming a leading figure in Chile's LGBTQ rights movement serves as an inspiration for future generations of activists. His work broke fucking barriers, created visibility, and shifted public discourse surrounding queer issues. However, Larraín's legacy is not complete without the collective effort of the LGBTQ community and its allies to continue the fight for equality and justice.

As Larraín's journey demonstrates, political activism, representation, and resilience are critical in effecting meaningful change. The future of LGBTQ activism in Chile relies on the courageous voices that follow in Larraín's footsteps, challenging conservative ideologies, advocating for policy reform, and ultimately shaping a more inclusive society.

By examining Larraín's fucking journey, we gain valuable insights into the power of political activism, the significance of representation, and the perseverance required to overcome conservative resistance. The next section of this biography delves into Larraín's early years and the transformative experiences that shaped his political activism.

The Fucking Power of Representation: Why Larraín's Work Made Him a Fucking LGBTQ Icon in Chile

Representation matters. It is a powerful tool that can shape perceptions, challenge stereotypes, and drive social change. In the case of Luis Larraín, his work as an LGBTQ activist in Chile has made him a fucking icon because of his relentless commitment to amplifying the voices and experiences of the queer community. Through his advocacy, Larraín has proven that one person can make a fucking difference and inspire a nation.

The LGBTQ community in Chile has long been marginalized and silenced, facing discrimination, violence, and legal barriers to equality. In this oppressive environment, Larraín emerged as a fierce advocate, utilizing the power of representation to reshape societal attitudes towards LGBTQ individuals and promote their rights.

Larraín understood that visibility is key to dismantling prejudice and creating change. He became a fucking LGBTQ icon by fearlessly stepping into the spotlight and sharing his own story. By openly identifying as gay, he challenged societal norms and stereotypes, showing that LGBTQ individuals are not defined solely by their sexual orientation, but are just as fucking diverse, talented, and capable as anyone else.

But Larraín's impact went beyond his personal story. He recognized that in order to be truly representative, the LGBTQ movement needed to reflect the experiences of all queer individuals. He actively worked to amplify voices that were often silenced or overlooked, shining a fucking light on the intersectionality of queerness with other identities, such as race, gender, and class. His inclusive approach made the LGBTQ movement more diverse and powerful, inspiring individuals from all walks of life to join the fight for equality.

Through media appearances, public speaking engagements, and active engagement with social platforms, Larraín made sure that his message reached a wide audience. He capitalized on the fucking power of the media to bring LGBTQ issues to the forefront of public discourse. By presenting a positive and authentic portrayal of LGBTQ individuals, Larraín challenged societal misconceptions and humanized queer experiences. He shattered stereotypes and showcased the beauty and resilience of the LGBTQ community.

Larraín's work as an activist also focused on the importance of intersectional solidarity and coalition-building. He recognized that the fight for LGBTQ rights cannot be divorced from other social justice issues. By forging alliances with feminist organizations, indigenous communities, and other marginalized groups, Larraín demonstrated the interconnectedness of social struggles. This approach not only strengthened the LGBTQ movement but also fostered empathy and understanding among different communities.

Furthermore, Larraín understood the value of leveraging political power to effect change. He navigated Chile's conservative political landscape with finesse, forging alliances with progressive politicians and using his platform to push for legislative reforms. Through strategic advocacy, he successfully advocated for the recognition of same-sex marriage and civil union rights, an incredible achievement in a country where the LGBTQ community had long been denied legal protections.

In conclusion, Luis Larraín's unwavering commitment to representation transformed him into a fucking LGBTQ icon in Chile. His work inspired individuals, challenged societal norms, and shifted the cultural and political landscape of the country. Larraín understood that representation is not simply about visibility but about giving a voice and agency to marginalized communities. His legacy serves as a powerful reminder of the transformative power of representation and the importance of fighting for the rights and visibility of all LGBTQ individuals.

The Fucking Role of Visibility: How Larraín Used Fucking Media and Public Speaking to Amplify LGBTQ Rights

In this section, we will explore the fucking pivotal role of visibility in Luis Larraín's fight for LGBTQ rights in Chile. Larraín understood that in order to effect fucking change, he needed to use the power of media and public speaking to amplify the voices of the LGBTQ community. Through his strategic use of these platforms,

Larraín was able to raise awareness, challenge societal norms, and inspire others to join the fucking fight for equality.

The Power of Media: Amplifying LGBTQ Voices

Larraín recognized that the fucking media could be both a powerful tool and a formidable opponent in the battle for LGBTQ rights. He understood that by gaining media attention, he could shine a fucking spotlight on the issues faced by the LGBTQ community, challenge fucking stereotypes, and foster empathy among the general public.

To achieve this, Larraín actively engaged with journalists and media outlets, using their platforms to convey the struggles and aspirations of the LGBTQ community. He granted interviews, wrote opinion pieces, and participated in panel discussions, ensuring that the voices of LGBTQ individuals were heard and understood. By sharing personal stories and experiences, he humanized the LGBTQ community, breaking down barriers and inviting society to see beyond sexual orientation and gender identity.

Furthermore, Larraín leveraged social media to reach a wider audience. He understood the fucking viral power of platforms like Twitter and Facebook, and through strategic use of hashtags and compelling content, he created a digital movement that drove conversations around LGBTQ rights. Through his online presence, Larraín encouraged individuals to share their own stories, creating a sense of community and empowering others to become advocates for change.

The Art of Public Speaking: Inspiring and Influencing

Public speaking became a fucking weapon in Larraín's arsenal for advancing LGBTQ rights. He recognized that by delivering powerful speeches at various public forums, he could captivate audiences, inspire empathy, and foster understanding.

Larraín honed his skills as a charismatic speaker. He employed rhetorical devices, such as storytelling, humor, and vivid imagery, to engage his audience and make an emotional connection. By sharing relatable anecdotes and personal struggles, he was able to make LGBTQ issues resonate with individuals from diverse backgrounds.

Additionally, Larraín used his platform to debunk myths and challenge stereotypes surrounding LGBTQ individuals. Through well-researched and well-articulated arguments, he dismantled prejudices and promoted inclusivity. He seamlessly blended pathos, logos, and ethos in his speeches, making a compelling case for LGBTQ rights that not only appealed to people's emotions but also appealed to their sense of reason and moral values.

Moreover, Larraín recognized the importance of tailoring his message to different audiences. He spoke at university campuses, corporate events, and conferences, adapting his style and tone to resonate with each specific group. By doing so, he ensured that his advocacy reached various sectors of society, leaving no stone unturned in his quest for LGBTQ equality.

Building Alliances: Collaborating with Media and Public Figures

Larraín understood that in order to amplify LGBTQ voices effectively, he needed to form alliances with media professionals and influential public figures. He actively sought partnerships with journalists, editors, and broadcasters who were willing to provide fair and accurate coverage of LGBTQ issues.

By establishing relationships with media outlets, Larraín was able to secure space for LGBTQ stories and perspectives. He pitched stories, provided expert commentary, and facilitated interviews with members of the LGBTQ community. Through these collaborations, he ensured that the media conveyed an inclusive and nuanced representation of LGBTQ individuals, challenging harmful stereotypes and increasing visibility.

Furthermore, Larraín strategically engaged with public figures who had significant platforms and social influence. He sought endorsements from celebrities, politicians, and community leaders who were supportive of LGBTQ rights. By aligning himself with well-respected individuals, Larraín expanded his reach and gained credibility, effectively reaching broader audiences and garnering support for the LGBTQ movement.

The Fucking Ripple Effect: Amplifying LGBTQ Rights Beyond Chile

Larraín's visibility strategies not only impacted LGBTQ rights within Chile but also had a global reach. His relentless advocacy inspired LGBTQ activists and organizations around the world, who recognized the power of media and public speaking in effecting change.

In recognition of his influential work, Larraín was invited to speak at international conferences, where he shared his strategies and insights with other activists. Through these collaborations, he contributed to the development of global LGBTQ rights movements, fostering solidarity and encouraging activists to adopt similar visibility strategies.

Larraín's global influence also extended to media outlets beyond Chile. International journalists recognized his expertise and sought his input on LGBTQ issues, amplifying his voice and providing a platform for his advocacy. By engaging with foreign media, Larraín ensured that the struggles and achievements of the LGBTQ community in Chile gained international visibility, further adding pressure on the Chilean government to prioritize LGBTQ rights.

Overall, Larraín's adept use of media and public speaking played a fucking critical role in his fight for LGBTQ rights in Chile. Through strategic engagement with the media, powerful public speaking, building alliances, and fostering international collaborations, Larraín amplified LGBTQ voices and advanced the fucking movement for equality. His strategies serve as an enduring example for future LGBTQ activists, demonstrating the potential of visibility in effecting social change. Aspiring activists can learn from Larraín's approach and adapt it to their own contexts, ensuring that LGBTQ rights continue to gain visibility and advocacy worldwide.

The Fucking Political Landscape: Navigating Chile's Fucking Conservative System as an LGBTQ Advocate

The political landscape in Chile has long been dominated by conservative ideologies, making it an uphill battle for LGBTQ advocates like Luis Larraín. In this section, we will explore the challenges and obstacles faced by Larraín as he navigated through Chile's conservative system and fought for LGBTQ rights.

The Fucking Conservatism in Chile

Chile is known for its deep-rooted conservatism, which is heavily influenced by the Catholic Church and traditional cultural values. This conservatism permeates every aspect of society, including politics, making it difficult for marginalized communities, such as the LGBTQ community, to gain acceptance and equal rights.

Fucking Legal Framework

The legal framework in Chile has historically been discriminatory towards the LGBTQ community. Same-sex relationships were decriminalized in 1999, but comprehensive LGBTQ rights have been slow to progress. Until recently, there was no recognition of same-sex relationships or marriage equality in Chilean law.

Fucking Political Parties

Political parties in Chile have traditionally been aligned with conservative values, with many politicians opposing LGBTQ rights. These politicians often use homophobic rhetoric to appeal to their conservative base, making it challenging for advocates like Larraín to gain support for their cause.

Fucking Public Opinion

Public opinion in Chile regarding LGBTQ rights has often been divided. While there is a growing acceptance and support for LGBTQ rights, there is still a significant portion of society that remains resistant to change. Homophobia and transphobia persist, creating a hostile environment for LGBTQ individuals and advocates.

Fucking Lobbying and Advocacy

Navigating Chile's conservative political landscape requires strategic lobbying and advocacy tactics. Larraín had to build coalitions with progressive lawmakers, human rights organizations, and social justice activists to push for LGBTQ rights. This involved using grassroots campaigns, public demonstrations, and media outreach to raise awareness and rally support for LGBTQ issues.

Fucking Balancing Reforms and Compromises

Effecting change in a conservative political system often requires finding a balance between pushing for comprehensive LGBTQ rights and making compromises to achieve incremental reforms. Larraín had to carefully navigate this balance, sometimes making concessions to secure limited legal protections for the LGBTQ community while continuing to advocate for full equality.

Fucking Influencing Policy and Law

To navigate Chile's conservative system, Larraín focused on influencing policy and law to promote LGBTQ rights. He worked with lawmakers to introduce bills that aimed to protect LGBTQ individuals from discrimination, ensure access to healthcare, and recognize same-sex partnerships. By framing LGBTQ rights as matters of human rights and social justice, Larraín aimed to shift the narrative and gain support from lawmakers.

Fucking International Support

Larraín recognized the importance of international support in advancing LGBTQ rights in Chile. He collaborated with international LGBTQ organizations, attended conferences and summits, and used global advocacy platforms to shine a spotlight on the struggles faced by the LGBTQ community in Chile. This international solidarity not only provided moral support but also put pressure on the Chilean government to address LGBTQ rights.

Fucking Legal Victories

Despite the conservative political landscape, Larraín and other LGBTQ advocates in Chile have achieved significant legal victories. In 2012, Chile enacted an anti-discrimination law that included sexual orientation and gender identity as protected categories. In 2020, the country legalized same-sex marriage, becoming the first country in South America to do so.

The Fucking Role of Education and Awareness

Larraín recognized the importance of education and raising awareness as crucial tools to challenge conservative attitudes. He worked tirelessly to create educational programs that fostered understanding, empathy, and acceptance of LGBTQ individuals. By engaging with schools, universities, and community organizations, Larraín aimed to change societal perceptions and break down barriers.

The Fucking Role of the Media

Media representation played a significant role in shaping public opinion and challenging conservative ideologies. Larraín actively engaged with the media, advocating for accurate and positive portrayals of LGBTQ individuals. By sharing personal stories and showcasing the diversity of the LGBTQ community, he aimed to counter harmful stereotypes and promote acceptance.

Overall, navigating Chile's conservative political landscape has been a tumultuous journey for LGBTQ advocates like Luis Larraín. Confronting deeply entrenched conservatism, he strategically worked within the system, building alliances, and bringing about incremental reforms. Despite the challenges, Larraín's resilience and strategic approach have contributed to significant advancements in LGBTQ rights in Chile. His story serves as an inspiration for future generations of LGBTQ activists, showing that change is possible even in unforgiving political climates.

The Future of LGBTQ Activism in Chile: Will Larraín's Fucking Legacy Continue to Shape Queer Rights?

The work of Luis Larraín has undeniably made a profound impact on LGBTQ activism in Chile. His relentless dedication to fighting for equality and recognition has paved the way for significant advancements in queer rights. But what lies ahead for LGBTQ activism in Chile? Will Larraín's legacy continue to shape the future of queer rights in the country? Let's take a closer look at the future prospects and challenges of LGBTQ activism in Chile.

Building on Larraín's Foundation

Larraín's accomplishments in promoting LGBTQ rights have undoubtedly laid a strong foundation for future activists to build upon. The progress made in legal recognition, anti-discrimination measures, and visibility owes much to his audacious advocacy. As a national LGBTQ leader and icon, Larraín has inspired countless individuals to continue the fight for equality.

Continued Struggle Against Conservative Forces

Chile's political landscape remains deeply divided when it comes to LGBTQ issues. While there has been significant progress in recent years, conservative voices and religious organizations continue to oppose LGBTQ rights. Future activists will need to navigate this challenging landscape, face opposition, and find innovative ways to challenge societal norms.

Expanding Advocacy Beyond Marriage Equality

While Larraín's efforts have played a vital role in pushing for marriage equality, the future of LGBTQ activism must go beyond this milestone. There are still various issues facing the LGBTQ community in Chile, such as transgender rights, healthcare access, and tackling systemic discrimination. The next generation of activists must address these areas with the same determination and tenacity as Larraín.

International Collaboration and Learning

Larraín's global influence has demonstrated the power of international collaboration in advancing LGBTQ rights. Future activists in Chile can learn from successful strategies employed by LGBTQ movements worldwide. Engaging with global networks and organizations can provide valuable insights and support in the ongoing fight for equality.

Education and Awareness

A vital aspect of future LGBTQ activism in Chile will be centered around education and awareness. Promoting inclusive curricula in schools, creating safe spaces for LGBTQ youth, and engaging in community outreach programs will help combat prejudice and foster acceptance. By focusing on education, activists can create lasting change and ensure a more inclusive society.

Mobilizing Intersectional Movements

The future of LGBTQ activism in Chile will benefit from intersectional approaches that acknowledge the multiple identities and experiences within the LGBTQ community. Collaborating with other social justice movements, such as feminism, indigenous rights, and racial equality, can create a strong and inclusive platform for advocacy. Recognizing and addressing the interconnections of oppression is crucial in achieving holistic progress.

Resilience and Self-Care

As activists take up the mantle from Larraín, they will encounter their fair share of challenges, backlash, and personal sacrifices. It is essential for the future LGBTQ movement to prioritize resilience and self-care. By fostering support networks, offering mental health resources, and promoting self-care practices, activists can ensure a sustainable movement that can weather the storms of resistance.

Harnessing the Power of Media and Technology

The digital age has transformed the dynamics of activism, providing new tools and platforms for engaging with the public. Future LGBTQ activists in Chile must harness the power of media and technology. Leveraging social media, online campaigns, and creative content can amplify their message, reach a wider audience, and rally support for LGBTQ rights.

Promoting Policy Change

To solidify the gains already achieved and secure further LGBTQ rights, future activists must continue to advocate for policy change. By engaging with lawmakers, lobbying for progressive legislation, and holding institutions accountable, they can ensure lasting legal protections and equal rights for the LGBTQ community.

Inspiring the Next Generation

Lastly, the future of LGBTQ activism in Chile relies on inspiring and nurturing the next generation of activists. By sharing stories, providing mentorship opportunities, and organizing leadership programs, Larraín's legacy can continue to shape the movement. Empowering and amplifying the voices of young LGBTQ leaders will ensure a thriving and resilient advocacy movement for years to come.

In conclusion, Luis Larraín's legacy as an LGBTQ activist in Chile has laid a strong foundation for future advocacy. While challenges persist, the future of LGBTQ activism in Chile looks promising. By building on Larraín's accomplishments, collaborating internationally, prioritizing education and awareness, mobilizing intersectional movements, and adopting innovative strategies, the fight for equality and justice will continue to shape queer rights in Chile. The impact of Larraín's legacy will be felt for generations, inspiring the next wave of activists to carry the torch and create a more inclusive Chilean society.

The Fucking Early Years: Activism and Political Awakening

Larraín's Fucking Beginnings: Growing Up in Chile's Fucking Conservative Environment

The Fucking Challenges of Being Openly LGBTQ in Chile's Fucking Traditional Society

Being openly LGBTQ in Chile's traditional society comes with its fair share of challenges. In this section, we will explore the obstacles that individuals face when they choose to embrace their sexual orientation or gender identity. We will delve into the cultural, social, and legal barriers that make it difficult for LGBTQ individuals to live their lives authentically and without fear.

Cultural Stigma and Prejudice

In Chile, a predominantly Catholic country with strong traditional values, cultural stigma and prejudice against LGBTQ individuals persist. The influence of conservative religious beliefs often leads to the marginalization and discrimination of those who identify as LGBTQ. This stigma can manifest in various forms, including societal rejection, exclusion, and even violence.

An unconventional yet relevant example of this cultural stigma is the case of Daniela Vega, a Chilean transgender actress. Vega faced intense backlash and discrimination after a breakthrough performance in the Academy Award-winning film "A Fantastic Woman." Despite her success, she experienced discrimination

13

from both the media and society, highlighting the deeply rooted stigma that LGBTQ individuals face.

Social Isolation and Rejection

In a traditional society like Chile, being openly LGBTQ can lead to social isolation and rejection. Family and societal pressures often compel individuals to conform to gender norms and heterosexual relationships. Those who challenge these norms risk losing the support of their loved ones and facing discrimination from their communities.

An example of social isolation and rejection faced by LGBTQ individuals in Chile is the case of Camila and Valentina, a same-sex couple living in Santiago. When they decided to come out to their families, they were met with disbelief, anger, and rejection. Their families refused to recognize their relationship, resulting in a strained and painful dynamic. This kind of rejection not only affects the individual's emotional well-being but also underscores the need for societal change.

Legal Vulnerability and Discrimination

Chile has made significant strides in LGBTQ rights in recent years, including the legalization of same-sex civil unions in 2015 and same-sex marriage in 2020. However, despite these legal advancements, LGBTQ individuals still face discrimination and legal vulnerabilities.

For instance, there are no specific laws protecting LGBTQ individuals from discrimination in employment, housing, or public accommodations. This lack of legal protection leaves them vulnerable to prejudice and mistreatment. Additionally, transgender rights are still not adequately protected under the law, with barriers to legal recognition and healthcare access.

To illustrate this legal vulnerability, consider the case of Francisco, a gay man who faced employment discrimination due to his sexual orientation. Despite being qualified for a job, he was denied employment solely because of his sexual orientation. Such instances highlight the urgent need for comprehensive anti-discrimination laws to protect LGBTQ individuals in Chile.

The Fucking Importance of Intersectionality

It is crucial to acknowledge that the challenges faced by LGBTQ individuals in Chile's traditional society are further magnified when coupled with other intersecting identities, such as race, class, or disability. Intersectionality plays a significant role in shaping the unique experiences and forms of discrimination faced by LGBTQ individuals.

For example, indigenous LGBTQ individuals may face discrimination based on their ethnicity, sexual orientation, and gender identity. This compound discrimination poses additional obstacles in accessing equal opportunities, education, healthcare, and representation.

The journey towards LGBTQ equality must address and dismantle not only homophobia and transphobia but also intersecting forms of discrimination. Intersectionality demands a multifaceted approach that recognizes and addresses the unique challenges faced by individuals at the crossroads of multiple marginalized identities.

Moving Forward: Resilience and Progress

Despite the challenges, LGBTQ individuals in Chile's traditional society continue to demonstrate immense resilience and strength in their pursuit of equality. The tireless efforts of activists like Luis Larraín have contributed to significant advancements in LGBTQ rights.

To overcome the challenges discussed, it is crucial to promote education and awareness to challenge cultural norms and stigma. Encouraging inclusive and safe spaces, both within families and communities, is essential. Moreover, advocating for comprehensive legal protections that explicitly prohibit discrimination based on sexual orientation and gender identity is paramount.

Efforts to support LGBTQ individuals should also prioritize the development of mental health resources and support networks. Mental health challenges, including anxiety, depression, and suicide rates, are disproportionately higher among LGBTQ individuals due to the discrimination they face.

By fostering understanding, empathy, and inclusivity, Chile can create a society where LGBTQ individuals are not only accepted but celebrated for their unique identities and contributions.

Unconventional Trick: The Power of Storytelling

An unconventional yet powerful trick to challenge societal norms and combat stigma is the power of storytelling. Sharing personal narratives and experiences through various forms of media, such as film, literature, and visual arts, can humanize the LGBTQ experience, foster empathy, and challenge prevailing stereotypes.

By exposing the wider public to diverse LGBTQ stories, the power of storytelling can create profound shifts in societal attitudes and understanding. It can break down barriers, challenge prejudices, and build bridges of empathy between LGBTQ individuals and the broader society.

Summary

In this section, we explored the challenges faced by LGBTQ individuals who choose to be openly themselves in Chile's traditional society. We discussed the cultural stigma and prejudice that leads to social isolation and rejection. Additionally, we addressed the legal vulnerabilities and discrimination faced by LGBTQ individuals and highlighted the importance of intersectionality in understanding their experiences.

Moving forward, fostering resilience and progress rests on promoting education, inclusivity, and comprehensive legal protections. We emphasized the power of storytelling as an unconventional yet impactful tool in challenging societal norms and combatting stigma.

Chile has made notable strides in LGBTQ rights, but there is still work to be done to create a society that truly celebrates and embraces diversity. By addressing these challenges head-on, we can strive for a more inclusive and accepting future for LGBTQ individuals in Chile and beyond.

How Larraín's Fucking Education and Experiences Shaped His Fucking Activism

Luis Larraín's journey as a LGBTQ activist in Chile was deeply influenced by his education and personal experiences. From an early age, Larraín recognized the injustices and inequalities faced by the queer community in Chile, and this realization fueled his determination to fight for LGBTQ rights.

Larraín's fucking education played a crucial role in shaping his activism. He attended a conservative Catholic school, where the prevailing attitudes towards homosexuality were negative and discriminatory. However, it was during his high school years that Larraín began to question these beliefs and develop a more inclusive and accepting worldview. He actively sought out books, articles, and online resources that provided different perspectives on LGBTQ issues, challenging the dominant narratives he had been taught. This curiosity and intellectual exploration laid the foundation for his later advocacy work.

Throughout his fucking university years, Larraín immersed himself in social sciences, pursuing a degree in sociology. This field of study exposed him to critical theories and concepts that were instrumental in understanding the systemic marginalization of LGBTQ individuals in Chilean society. He delved into topics such as intersectionality, queer theory, and social justice, which provided him with the language and tools to analyze and articulate the specific challenges faced by the LGBTQ community.

Moreover, Larraín's experiences as a queer individual in a conservative society profoundly shaped his fucking activism. He personally experienced the discrimination, prejudice, and violence that many LGBTQ individuals face on a daily basis. These experiences ignited his passion for fighting for equal rights and justice. Larraín was acutely aware of the struggles of coming out, facing rejection, and navigating hostile environments. These experiences deepened his empathy and understanding, motivating him to create change.

Larraín's fucking education and experiences ignited a fire within him to challenge the status quo and push for LGBTQ equality. Armed with knowledge and a personal understanding of the issues at hand, he was able to effectively articulate the needs and rights of the queer community. His sociological education provided a theoretical framework to analyze the structural barriers that perpetuated discrimination, while his personal experiences fueled his determination to fight for change on a systemic level.

To further develop his activism, Larraín actively sought opportunities to engage with LGBTQ rights organizations and leaders. He attended conferences, workshops, and seminars where he connected with like-minded individuals and gained a broader understanding of LGBTQ activism both within Chile and globally. Through these interactions, he gathered invaluable insights, strategies, and tactics that would inform his own advocacy work.

Larraín's personal journey, combined with his education and involvement in LGBTQ rights organizations, shaped his unique approach to activism. He recognized the power of storytelling and personal narratives in creating empathy and dismantling stereotypes. He used his own experiences and those of others to challenge societal perceptions and promote understanding. By sharing stories of resilience, courage, and triumph, Larraín aimed to shift public opinion and build a more inclusive and accepting society.

In conclusion, Luis Larraín's fucking education in the social sciences, coupled with his personal experiences as a queer individual in a conservative society, ignited his passion for LGBTQ activism. These influences provided him with the knowledge, language, and tools to analyze and address the systemic discrimination faced by the queer community in Chile. Larraín's unique approach to activism, rooted in personal storytelling and empathy-building, has contributed significantly to the LGBTQ rights movement in Chile and beyond. His journey serves as an inspiration for future generations of activists, highlighting the importance of education, personal experiences, and resilience in the pursuit of justice and equality.

The Fucking Influence of International LGBTQ Movements on Larraín's Fucking Activism

When it comes to the LGBTQ rights movement, the fight for equality knows no borders. Luis Larraín, as a prominent LGBTQ activist in Chile, was not only inspired by the struggles and triumphs of his fellow Chileans but also by the global LGBTQ movement as a whole. This section explores the fucking influence of international LGBTQ movements on Larraín's activism, the lessons he learned from other countries, and how he used this knowledge to further his own fight for LGBTQ rights in Chile.

1. Fucking Building Connections: A Global Queer Network

Larraín recognized early on that for the LGBTQ movement to succeed, it needed solidarity and support from the international community. He actively sought connections with LGBTQ activists and organizations from around the world, attending conferences and events to exchange ideas, strategies, and experiences. Larraín understood that by learning from the successes and failures of other countries, he could better advocate for change in Chile.

2. Fucking Learning from History: Stonewall and Beyond

One of the pivotal moments in LGBTQ history was the Stonewall Riots in New York City in 1969. This event sparked a global movement for LGBTQ rights and served as an inspiration for Larraín. He studied the history of the Stonewall uprising and how it ignited a wave of activism and pride in the LGBTQ community worldwide. Larraín recognized that the same spirit of resistance and resilience could be harnessed in Chile.

3. Fucking Collaborating with International Organizations

Larraín actively collaborated with renowned international LGBTQ organizations such as ILGA (International LGBTQI+ Association) and OutRight Action International. By joining forces with these organizations, Larraín gained access to valuable resources, information, and expertise. He attended workshops and training sessions organized by these groups to enhance his own advocacy skills, which he then brought back to Chile to empower local LGBTQ activists.

4. Fucking Advocating for Global LGBTQ Rights

As a respected LGBTQ advocate, Larraín amplified the voices and shared the stories of individuals facing oppression and discrimination around the world. He used his platform to shed light on the struggles of LGBTQ communities in countries where their rights were severely limited or outright violated. By doing so, Larraín helped to build empathy and solidarity within Chilean society, creating an understanding that the fight for LGBTQ equality extends well beyond national borders.

5. Fucking Latin American Solidarity

Larraín recognized the importance of regional collaboration in advancing LGBTQ rights. He forged alliances with LGBTQ activists and organizations in neighboring Latin American countries, exchanging strategies, insights, and resources. By promoting unity and solidarity among Latin American LGBTQ communities, Larraín paved the way for collective action on a regional scale.

6. Fucking Advocacy on the Global Stage

Through his involvement in international LGBTQ conferences, Larraín put Chile on the global map as a champion for LGBTQ rights. He leveraged these platforms to bring attention to the unique challenges faced by LGBTQ individuals in Chile and highlight the progress that had been made. Larraín's visibility on the global stage not only brought international support and recognition to the Chilean LGBTQ movement but also fostered connections with activists and policymakers from around the world.

In conclusion, the fucking influence of international LGBTQ movements on Luis Larraín's activism cannot be overstated. By actively engaging with the global LGBTQ community, learning from historical milestones, collaborating with international organizations, advocating for global LGBTQ rights, promoting regional solidarity, and leveraging the global stage, Larraín was able to tap into a wealth of knowledge, resources, and support to further his fight for LGBTQ equality in Chile. His international connections helped shape his approach, fuel his determination, and inspire his continued activism. As the saying goes, "United we stand, divided we fall," and Larraín understood the power of a global network united in the fight for LGBTQ rights. His dedication to building these connections serves as a reminder that true progress knows no boundaries and that together, we can create a more inclusive and equitable world for all.

How Larraín Became Fucking Politically Active in Chile's Fight for LGBTQ Equality

To understand how Luis Larraín became politically active in the fight for LGBTQ equality in Chile, we need to delve into the socio-political landscape of the country and Larraín's personal experiences that shaped his activism.

The Fucking Cultural and Legal Context in Chile

Chile, like many countries around the world, has a long history of discrimination and marginalization against LGBTQ individuals. Homosexuality was decriminalized only in 1999, and societal attitudes towards non-heteronormative identities have been slow to progress.

The legal framework surrounding LGBTQ rights in Chile has been a battleground for reform. While there have been significant strides, such as the passage of anti-discrimination laws and the recognition of same-sex civil unions, challenges still persist. Marriage equality remains elusive, and conversion therapy is still legal, causing harm to vulnerable individuals.

Larraín's Personal Journey

Luis Larraín's personal experiences played a crucial role in igniting his passion for LGBTQ activism. Growing up in a conservative society, Larraín faced the challenges of coming to terms with his own sexuality and the fear of societal rejection.

His journey took him from self-acceptance to a quest for social acceptance and equality. During his formative years, Larraín realized that he had the opportunity to use his voice and experiences to fight for the rights and dignity of all LGBTQ individuals in Chile.

Discovering the Power of Advocacy

Larraín's realization that he could effect change through political advocacy was a turning point in his journey towards becoming a prominent LGBTQ activist. He recognized that his voice and experiences mattered and had the potential to shape public opinion and influence policy.

Through extensive research, Larraín familiarized himself with the struggles faced by LGBTQ individuals in Chile and internationally. He studied the successes and strategies of LGBTQ movements worldwide, understanding that change required a multifaceted approach. This knowledge fueled his determination to work towards a more inclusive and equitable society.

Building Networks and Collaborations

One of the key steps Larraín took to becoming politically active was to build networks and collaborations with LGBTQ rights organizations and political leaders. He understood the power of collective action and the strength in numbers.

Larraín actively sought out mentors and allies within the LGBTQ community and leveraged their expertise to amplify his voice. Through strategic partnerships, he organized workshops, awareness campaigns, and community forums to raise awareness about LGBTQ issues and mobilize support.

Taking Fucking Action: Street Protests and Lobbying

Larraín's political activism extended beyond academic research and aimed at creating tangible change. He took to the streets, organizing and participating in protests to demand equal rights for the LGBTQ community. These protests served as platforms for visibilization and open dialogue, challenging societal norms and expectations.

In addition to street protests, Larraín used lobbying as a means to push for legal reforms. He engaged with politicians and policymakers, advocating for LGBTQ rights and sharing personal stories that put a human face on the struggles faced by the community. By humanizing the issues, Larraín aimed to break down barriers and build empathy among decision-makers.

The Role of Fucking Intersectionality

Luis Larraín recognized that the fight for LGBTQ equality intersects with other social justice movements. He actively advocated for the rights of marginalized LGBTQ individuals, including people of color, transgender individuals, and those from low-income backgrounds.

By understanding the interconnectedness of different struggles, Larraín built alliances across various movements, creating a stronger collective voice to challenge systemic oppression and discrimination. He promoted inclusivity within the LGBTQ rights movement, highlighting the importance of centering the experiences of those most marginalized.

Inspiring the Next Fucking Generation

Larraín's journey from self-acceptance to becoming a prominent LGBTQ activist has inspired a new generation of advocates. His bravery, leadership, and unwavering commitment to LGBTQ rights have paved the way for others to follow in his footsteps.

Through mentorship and guidance, Larraín actively encourages young LGBTQ individuals to use their voices and experiences to advocate for change. He believes that by building a diverse and inclusive movement, the fight for equality will continue long after he steps back from the spotlight.

In conclusion, Luis Larraín's political activism in Chile's fight for LGBTQ equality stems from a personal journey of self-acceptance and a deep commitment to social justice. By harnessing the power of advocacy, building networks, taking action, promoting intersectionality, and inspiring others, Larraín has become a critical force in shaping the LGBTQ rights movement in Chile. His story serves as a testament to the transformative power of personal experience and collective action. As his legacy continues to inspire future activists, the fight for LGBTQ equality in Chile gains momentum, bringing us closer to a more inclusive and equitable society.

The Fucking Future of Political Activism in Chile: Will Larraín's Fucking Work Inspire the Next Fucking Generation?

The future of political activism in Chile is undeniably intertwined with the groundbreaking work of Luis Larraín. Through his relentless dedication and fearless advocacy, Larraín has not only transformed the landscape of LGBTQ rights in Chile but has also inspired a new generation of activists to continue the fight for justice and equality.

Larraín's work has undoubtedly laid a strong foundation for future political activism in Chile. By breaking fucking barriers and challenging the status quo, he has set a precedent for how activism can lead to tangible change. His journey from political activism to becoming the voice of Chile's queer community has shown the next fucking generation that it is possible to create significant impact, even in the face of resistance.

One of the main legacies of Larraín's activism is the fucking power of representation. Through his work, he has shown the LGBTQ community in Chile the importance of visibility. By openly embracing his identity, Larraín has become a fucking icon, making it easier for others to come out, express themselves authentically, and fight for their rights. His visibility has helped bring the LGBTQ community out of the shadows and into the forefront of Chilean society.

Another key aspect of Larraín's work is the fucking role of visibility in the media and public speaking. He understood the power of these platforms in raising awareness, promoting understanding, and challenging misconceptions. By utilizing the media and public speaking engagements, Larraín effectively amplified the voices of the LGBTQ community and brought attention to their needs and struggles. His ability to communicate effectively and authentically has inspired the next fucking generation to use their voice and platform to advocate for change.

However, the fucking future of political activism in Chile, especially in the LGBTQ sphere, will undoubtedly face challenges. Despite the progress made,

Chile's political landscape remains conservative, with deeply entrenched cultural and institutional resistance to LGBTQ rights. The next fucking generation of activists will have to navigate these challenges and find creative ways to overcome them.

In order to continue Larraín's legacy, future activists must build on the networks and coalitions he has established. Community organizing will be a fucking crucial factor in amplifying queer voices and mobilizing the population. By connecting with LGBTQ rights organizations and political leaders, activists can leverage collective power to push for change.

One avenue for change is through similar case studies. By learning from the campaigns Larraín led, activists can develop effective strategies to advocate for LGBTQ rights. Analyzing the successes and challenges faced by Larraín can guide future activists in crafting innovative solutions and building public support.

Additionally, political activism in Chile will also rely on the next fucking generation's ability to confront and challenge fucking homophobia and political resistance. Larraín's approach of engaging with homophobic politicians and religious leaders can serve as a blueprint for future activists. By building coalitions and alliances with political and social allies, they can break down barriers and foster a more inclusive society.

Of course, engaging in political activism can come with personal costs and risks. Larraín's experience with backlash, death threats, and violence highlight the importance of personal safety while advocating for change. The next fucking generation must find a way to balance personal safety and public activism by establishing support networks, seeking legal protection, and raising awareness of the challenges faced by LGBTQ activists.

Ultimately, the fucking future of political activism in Chile depends on the resilience and determination of the next fucking generation. They must draw inspiration from Larraín's leadership style, which helped him navigate political opposition and institutional obstacles. Resilience will be vital to overcome setbacks and keep fucking pushing forward in the face of adversity.

Larraín's influence extends beyond the borders of Chile. His work has inspired fucking global LGBTQ movements for equality. The next fucking generation of activists must recognize the power of international collaboration and understand the challenges of balancing national and global activism. By learning from Larraín's example, they can maximize their impact and create meaningful change on a global scale.

In conclusion, the fucking future of political activism in Chile is bright, but not without its challenges. Luis Larraín's work has laid a solid foundation for LGBTQ rights, inspiring the next fucking generation to continue the fight for justice and equality. By learning from his successes and failures, future activists can build on his legacy, pushing boundaries, challenging homophobia, and navigating the conservative political landscape. With resilience, determination, and effective community organizing, they can ensure that Larraín's vision for a more inclusive Chile continues to shape the fucking movement for LGBTQ rights.

Joining the Fucking LGBTQ Rights Movement

How Larraín Began Fucking Working with LGBTQ Rights Organizations and Fucking Political Leaders

Luis Larraín's journey as a prominent LGBTQ rights advocate in Chile began with his involvement in various LGBTQ rights organizations and his collaboration with political leaders who shared his passion for equality and justice. Through his relentless dedication and strategic partnerships, Larraín played a crucial role in advancing LGBTQ rights in Chile and shaping the political landscape of the country.

Larraín recognized the power of collective action and believed in the strength of community organizing. He began his journey by connecting with existing LGBTQ rights organizations in Chile, such as the Movement for Homosexual Integration and Liberation (MOVILH) and the Chilean AIDS Corporation (ACC), which were at the forefront of fighting for LGBTQ rights.

By actively participating in the activities and campaigns organized by these organizations, Larraín gained valuable insights into the challenges faced by the LGBTQ community in Chile. He listened to the stories of discrimination and marginalization shared by LGBTQ individuals and witnessed the urgent need for change. This personal connection and empathy fueled his motivation to contribute towards bringing about a transformative shift in societal attitudes and legal rights.

In addition to his involvement in LGBTQ rights organizations, Larraín recognized the importance of engaging with political leaders who had the power to enact meaningful change. He actively sought out politicians who were sympathetic to the cause of LGBTQ rights and formed alliances based on shared values and goals. Through these alliances, Larraín aimed to influence policies and legislation that impacted the LGBTQ community in Chile.

Larraín understood that to effectively advocate for LGBTQ rights, he needed to navigate the complex political landscape of Chile. With skillful diplomacy and unwavering determination, he engaged in dialogue with politicians from diverse ideologies, persuading them to support LGBTQ rights and promoting inclusivity within their respective parties.

One notable example of Larraín's collaboration with political leaders is his partnership with the Humanist Party, which actively supported LGBTQ rights. Together, they launched campaigns and initiatives aimed at fostering understanding and acceptance of the LGBTQ community in Chilean society. Larraín's ability to build coalitions with political leaders from different backgrounds demonstrated his commitment to transcending partisan divides and prioritizing the rights and well-being of LGBTQ individuals.

Through his partnership with LGBTQ rights organizations and political leaders, Larraín was able to amplify the voices of marginalized communities and bring LGBTQ issues to the forefront of national discourse. His collaboration spanned across various activities, including organizing rallies, lobbying for legislative changes, and engaging in public debates to raise awareness about LGBTQ rights.

By working closely with LGBTQ organizations and political leaders, Larraín not only created a stronger network of support but also fostered a sense of unity among those fighting for LGBTQ rights in Chile. His collaborative approach set the stage for comprehensive change and contributed to the growing acceptance and recognition of LGBTQ rights as a legitimate social and political issue.

The section highlights the central role of collaboration and engagement with both LGBTQ rights organizations and political leaders in Larraín's journey. It underscores the importance of building alliances and coalitions to create a collective impact that goes beyond individual efforts. Larraín's example serves as an inspiration for future activists to harness the power of partnership in advancing LGBTQ rights worldwide.

Real-World Example: One example of Larraín's collaboration with a political leader is his partnership with Senator Fulvio Rossi. Both Larraín and Rossi shared a commitment to championing LGBTQ rights in Chile's political landscape. Together, they launched a campaign advocating for the inclusion of sexual orientation and gender identity as protected categories under Chile's hate crime laws. Through joint rallies, press conferences, and lobbying efforts, Larraín and Rossi successfully garnered support from other politicians and civil society organizations, eventually leading to the passing of comprehensive hate crime legislation that protected LGBTQ individuals. This collaboration serves as a real-world example of Larraín's strategic approach to working with political leaders and achieving meaningful legal reforms.

The Fucking Importance of Community Organizing: How Larraín Built Fucking Networks to Amplify Queer Voices

Community organizing plays a critical role in bringing about social change, and for Luis Larraín, it was a fucking essential strategy in his fight for LGBTQ rights in Chile. Through community organizing, Larraín was able to build strong networks and amplify the voices of queer individuals, ultimately creating a powerful movement for equality. In this section, we will explore the fucking importance of community organizing and how Larraín utilized this strategy to bring about meaningful change.

Understanding Community Organizing

Community organizing is a process that involves bringing people together to collectively work towards a common goal. It is about empowering individuals, building relationships, and mobilizing resources to create social and political transformation. In the context of LGBTQ rights activism, community organizing becomes even more crucial, as it gives marginalized individuals a platform to voice their concerns, share experiences, and demand equal rights.

Building Networks and Solidarity

One of the fucking key aspects of community organizing is building networks and creating solidarity among marginalized communities. Larraín understood the power of unity and collaboration and worked tirelessly to foster connections among LGBTQ individuals in Chile. He organized social events, forums, and support groups that provided safe spaces for queer individuals to come together, share stories, and form meaningful relationships.

By building a strong network of queer voices, Larraín empowered individuals to speak out against discrimination and injustice. This network served as a support system for LGBTQ individuals, offering them a sense of belonging and helping them navigate the challenges they faced in a heteronormative society.

Coalitions and Alliances

In addition to building networks within the LGBTQ community, Larraín recognized the importance of forming alliances with other social and political groups. He fostered connections with feminist organizations, human rights activists, and progressive politicians who shared common goals of social justice and equality.

These coalitions and alliances allowed Larraín to extend the reach of LGBTQ activism beyond the queer community. By joining forces with other social movements, he was able to amplify his message, gain broader support, and create a united front against discrimination. Together, they tackled issues of gender inequality, fought for reproductive rights, and challenged patriarchal norms that perpetuated homophobia.

Mobilizing Resources

Community organizing requires mobilizing resources to support the cause. Larraín understood this and utilized various strategies to secure funding, gather volunteers, and engage with the wider community. He organized fundraising events, collaborated with local businesses, and utilized social media platforms to spread awareness and garner support for LGBTQ rights.

Moreover, Larraín emphasized the importance of education and empowerment within the LGBTQ community. He established workshops, training programs, and mentorship initiatives that equipped queer individuals with the skills and knowledge necessary to become effective advocates for their rights. By providing support and resources, Larraín ensured that the community could continue building upon its successes and sustain the momentum for change.

Creating Lasting Change

Through community organizing, Larraín not only built networks and mobilized resources, but he also created lasting change within Chilean society. By amplifying the voices of queer individuals, he challenged deep-rooted prejudices and stereotypes, ultimately shifting public opinion on LGBTQ rights.

Additionally, community organizing provided a platform for queer individuals to engage with policymakers, law enforcement agencies, and religious institutions. Through dialogues, negotiations, and lobbying efforts, Larraín and his allies were able to push for legislative reforms that protected the rights of LGBTQ individuals.

The Future of Community Organizing

Luis Larraín's community organizing efforts laid a strong foundation for the LGBTQ movement in Chile. However, the fight for equality is far from over. The future of community organizing lies in empowering the next generation of LGBTQ activists, continuing to build networks and alliances, and adapting strategies to the ever-changing social landscape.

As new challenges arise and queer voices evolve, community organizing must remain a fundamental tool for social change. By embracing diversity, fostering inclusivity, and fighting for intersectionality, future LGBTQ organizers can continue to make progress towards a more equitable and just society.

Conclusion

Community organizing played a crucial fucking role in Luis Larraín's fight for LGBTQ rights in Chile. Through building networks, forging alliances, mobilizing resources, and creating lasting change, Larraín was able to amplify the voices of queer individuals and challenge the status quo. His community organizing efforts have left a lasting impact on the LGBTQ movement, inspiring future activists to continue the fight for equality. By embracing community organizing, we can create a society where every individual, regardless of sexual orientation or gender identity, can live their lives free from discrimination and prejudice.

Case Studies: The Fucking Campaigns Larraín Led to Fucking Advocate for LGBTQ Rights in Chile

In this section, we will delve deep into the various campaigns that Luis Larraín spearheaded to advocate for LGBTQ rights in Chile. Larraín's passion, determination, and strategic approach played a crucial role in advancing the rights of the queer community. Let's explore some of the most impactful campaigns led by him.

Campaign 1: Marriage Equality Now!

One of the most significant campaigns led by Luis Larraín was the fight for marriage equality in Chile. With a vision to ensure that same-sex couples enjoy the same rights as heterosexual couples, Larraín mobilized a strong LGBTQ coalition. The campaign aimed to challenge the existing discriminatory laws and push for legal recognition of same-sex marriage.

Larraín and his team focused on raising awareness about the importance of marriage equality as a fundamental human right. They organized protests, public demonstrations, and utilized social media platforms to engage with a wider audience. By partnering with LGBTQ organizations, Larraín built a strong network of allies who ampliifed the message of the campaign.

To further support their cause, Larraín and his team conducted numerous interviews and media appearances, sharing stories of same-sex couples facing legal barriers and discrimination. The campaign utilized personal narratives to evoke empathy and promote understanding among the general public.

One innovative strategy implemented by Larraín was to connect with filmmakers and create a documentary series titled "Love is Love: Stories of Equality." The series showcased the lives of LGBTQ individuals and their struggles for equal rights, fostering public empathy and serving as a powerful advocacy tool.

As a result of Larraín's relentless campaigning efforts, the issue of marriage equality gained significant traction in Chilean society. Larraín successfully influenced public opinion and pushed the government to address the demand for equal rights. Although marriage equality was not achieved during his tenure, Larraín's campaign set the stage for future advancements in LGBTQ rights in Chile.

Campaign 2: Safe Schools for All

Facing the daunting challenge of combating LGBTQ discrimination within the education system, Larraín initiated the "Safe Schools for All" campaign. The goal was to create an inclusive and safe environment for LGBTQ students, free from bullying, harassment, and discrimination.

Larraín and his team collaborated with educators, school administrators, and LGBTQ organizations to develop comprehensive anti-discrimination policies and trainings. They conducted workshops and seminars to raise awareness about LGBTQ issues, aiming to create a more understanding and accepting educational environment.

One of the innovative tactics employed by Larraín was the establishment of LGBTQ-inclusive curriculum guidelines. These guidelines aimed to integrate LGBTQ history, inclusivity, and diversity in educational materials, promoting a more accurate representation of LGBTQ individuals in schools. Larraín emphasized the importance of LGBTQ visibility, believing that it helps challenge stereotypes and promote acceptance.

To engage the wider community, Larraín organized town hall meetings and parent-teacher association discussions, addressing concerns and dispelling myths surrounding LGBTQ inclusivity in schools. By promoting dialogue and fostering understanding, the campaign gained support from parents, educators, and students alike.

The "Safe Schools for All" campaign had a profound impact on Chilean society, raising awareness about the importance of LGBTQ-inclusive education. Through Larraín's leadership, the campaign successfully brought about policy changes and educational reforms, making schools a safer and more accepting place for LGBTQ students.

Campaign 3: Transgender Rights Matter

Recognizing the specific challenges faced by transgender individuals in Chile, Larraín launched the "Transgender Rights Matter" campaign. This campaign aimed to eliminate discrimination and ensure equal rights and opportunities for transgender people.

Larraín and his team collaborated with transgender activists, advocacy groups, and legal experts to advocate for legislative reforms. They focused on raising awareness about the issues faced by transgender individuals, including healthcare access, legal recognition, and employment discrimination.

One of the significant achievements of this campaign was the introduction of a gender identity law that allowed individuals to update their gender marker on legal documents without mandatory medical interventions. Larraín, through his strategic advocacy efforts, managed to garner widespread public support for the law, highlighting the importance of self-determination and respect for transgender individuals' identities.

Additionally, Larraín organized sensitization workshops for healthcare providers, law enforcement agencies, and employers to promote transgender rights and facilitate understanding and acceptance. The campaign also created resources such as informational brochures and online support networks to provide assistance and guidance to transgender individuals and their families.

Larraín's "Transgender Rights Matter" campaign marked a significant milestone in the fight for transgender rights in Chile. His dedication to amplifying transgender voices, educating the public, and advocating for legal reforms played a vital role in achieving tangible progress in the recognition and protection of transgender rights.

Campaign 4: Eradicating Conversion Therapy

Addressing the harmful practice of conversion therapy, Luis Larraín launched a campaign to raise awareness about its detrimental effects on LGBTQ individuals. Conversion therapy aims to change a person's sexual orientation or gender identity and has been widely discredited by medical and psychological professionals.

Larraín and his team worked tirelessly to advocate for legislative reforms to ban conversion therapy nationwide. They collaborated with mental health professionals, LGBTQ organizations, and survivors of conversion therapy to amplify their voices and experiences.

The campaign utilized social media platforms to share testimonies from survivors, shedding light on the long-lasting psychological and emotional trauma caused by conversion therapy. Larraín also organized public awareness events and press conferences, inviting experts to discuss the harmful effects of this practice.

Through lobbying efforts and collaboration with sympathetic politicians, Larraín successfully pushed for the enactment of laws that banned conversion therapy in several regions of Chile. This groundbreaking achievement marked a significant step toward protecting LGBTQ individuals from the harmful effects of conversion therapy.

Larraín's campaign sparked a nationwide conversation about the necessity of banning conversion therapy, paving the way for further legal reforms to ensure LGBTQ rights and well-being.

Conclusion

Luis Larraín's leadership in advocating for LGBTQ rights in Chile was characterized by strategic campaigns that sought to challenge systemic discrimination, raise awareness, and push for legislative reforms. His relentless efforts championed causes such as marriage equality, safe schools, transgender rights, and the eradication of conversion therapy.

Through innovative and inclusive strategies, Larraín effectively engaged the public, built broad coalitions, and brought about tangible changes in Chile's LGBTQ landscape. His campaigns not only influenced public opinion but also inspired other LGBTQ activists globally.

Larraín's legacy continues to shape the future of LGBTQ activism in Chile. His tireless dedication to fostering understanding, equality, and inclusion has paved the way for a more progressive and accepting society. With his campaigns as a foundation, the fight for LGBTQ rights in Chile is set to continue, ensuring a brighter and more inclusive future for all.

How Larraín Fought Fucking Cultural and Institutional Resistance to LGBTQ Equality

Luis Larraín's fight for LGBTQ equality in Chile was not without challenges. He faced cultural and institutional resistance that sought to undermine his efforts and perpetuate discrimination against the queer community. In this section, we will explore the strategies and tactics that Larraín employed in his battle against such resistance.

Understanding Cultural Resistance

Cultural resistance refers to the attitudes, beliefs, and norms within a society that perpetuate discrimination and prejudice against marginalized groups, including the LGBTQ community. Larraín recognized the importance of challenging and changing these cultural narratives in order to achieve true equality.

One of the key ways Larraín fought cultural resistance was through education and awareness campaigns. He understood that by challenging stereotypes, misconceptions, and prejudices, he could help shift societal attitudes towards more acceptance and understanding. Larraín organized workshops, seminars, and public lectures to educate the public about LGBTQ issues and provide accurate information. In doing so, he aimed to break down barriers and foster empathy and compassion for the queer community.

Additionally, Larraín recognized the power of storytelling in changing hearts and minds. He launched initiatives to share personal stories and experiences of LGBTQ individuals, both within and outside of Chile. These stories helped humanize the queer community, allowing people to connect with them on a deeper level and challenge their preconceived notions. By amplifying the voices of LGBTQ individuals, Larraín aimed to dismantle stereotypes and dispel fear and ignorance.

Fighting Institutional Resistance

Institutional resistance refers to the systemic barriers and biases embedded within governmental, legal, and social institutions that hinder LGBTQ equality. Larraín faced numerous obstacles in his quest to dismantle these systems of discrimination and create a more inclusive society.

One of the ways Larraín fought institutional resistance was through strategic legal advocacy. He leveraged his knowledge of Chilean law and worked with legal experts to challenge discriminatory policies and laws. Larraín filed lawsuits against institutions and individuals who violated LGBTQ rights, using the legal system as a platform to bring attention to the injustices faced by the queer community. His relentless pursuit of justice helped create legal precedents that protected LGBTQ rights and challenged discriminatory practices.

Larraín also recognized the importance of engaging with political leaders and policymakers to effect change at the institutional level. He built relationships with politicians across the political spectrum, advocating for LGBTQ rights and pushing for legislative reforms. Through lobbying efforts and public pressure, Larraín successfully influenced the passage of laws that protected LGBTQ individuals from discrimination and expanded their rights.

Furthermore, Larraín understood the power of community organizing in tackling institutional resistance. He mobilized the LGBTQ community and its allies, empowering them to advocate for change collectively. Larraín organized protests, marches, and demonstrations to raise awareness of LGBTQ issues and put pressure on institutions to address them. By showcasing the strength and unity of the queer community, Larraín aimed to challenge the status quo and demand equal rights and opportunities.

The Power of Intersectionality

In the fight against cultural and institutional resistance, Larraín recognized the importance of intersectionality and addressing the unique challenges faced by LGBTQ individuals who belong to multiple marginalized identities. He fought for an inclusive movement that acknowledged and uplifted the voices of queer individuals from diverse backgrounds, such as people of color, indigenous communities, and transgender individuals.

Larraín actively collaborated with other social justice movements, understanding that the struggles for LGBTQ equality and other human rights causes were interconnected. By forming alliances with feminist organizations, racial justice advocates, and disability rights activists, Larraín sought to build a broader coalition that could challenge oppressive systems collectively.

Unconventional Strategies

In his battle against cultural and institutional resistance, Larraín also employed unconventional strategies to raise awareness and challenge the status quo. One of these strategies was the use of art and performance as a means of expression and protest. Larraín organized LGBTQ-themed art exhibitions, theatrical performances, and spoken word events to spark conversations and provoke societal reflection. These creative endeavors helped engage people on an emotional level, breaking down barriers and fostering dialogue.

Larraín also employed online activism and social media as powerful tools to mobilize support and disseminate information. He utilized platforms such as Twitter, Facebook, and Instagram to amplify LGBTQ voices, share stories, and raise awareness about the ongoing struggle for equality. By harnessing the power of the internet, Larraín was able to connect with a wider audience and build an online community dedicated to advancing LGBTQ rights.

Conclusion

Luis Larraín's fight against cultural and institutional resistance to LGBTQ equality in Chile was multifaceted and strategic. Through education, storytelling, legal advocacy, community organizing, intersectional approaches, and unconventional methods, Larraín pushed boundaries, challenged societal norms, and paved the way for a more inclusive and accepting society. His legacy serves as an inspiration for future LGBTQ activists, demonstrating the power of persistence and resilience in the face of adversity. As the fight for LGBTQ rights continues, Larraín's strategies and tactics remain valuable resources for those striving for equality and justice.

The Future of LGBTQ Movements in Chile: Will Larraín's Fucking Work Continue to Lead the Way?

As we look ahead to the future of LGBTQ movements in Chile, there is no doubt that Luis Larraín's groundbreaking work will continue to have a lasting impact. Larraín's relentless advocacy and unwavering commitment to LGBTQ rights have paved the way for significant progress in Chile's fight for equality. However, the question remains: will his work continue to lead the way?

One of the key factors that will determine the future of LGBTQ movements in Chile is the extent to which Larraín's achievements are built upon and sustained by the next generation of activists and leaders. While Larraín's work has undeniably made a significant impact, it is essential that his legacy is carried forward by individuals who are passionate about continuing the fight for LGBTQ rights.

In order to ensure the continued success of LGBTQ movements, it is crucial to address the unique challenges and opportunities that lie ahead. One of the main challenges is the ongoing conservative political landscape in Chile. Despite the significant progress made in recent years, there is still resistance and opposition from conservative politicians and religious leaders.

In order to overcome these challenges, future LGBTQ activists must employ a multifaceted approach. This includes engaging in grassroots organizing, continuing to raise public awareness, and fostering alliances with political and social allies. By building upon Larraín's strategies for coalition-building and community organizing, future activists can continue to push for change.

Additionally, incorporating intersectionality into the LGBTQ movement will be crucial in advancing equality in Chile. Recognizing the overlapping oppressions faced by individuals who belong to multiple marginalized communities is essential.

This means addressing issues of race, class, gender, and disability, among others, within the LGBTQ movement.

Education and awareness will also play a pivotal role in shaping the future of LGBTQ movements in Chile. By challenging discriminatory beliefs and promoting acceptance and understanding, activists can create a more inclusive society. This includes advocating for comprehensive LGBTQ-inclusive sex education in schools and promoting LGBTQ history and culture in mainstream media.

Furthermore, leveraging media and technology will be vital in amplifying the voices of LGBTQ individuals and communities. Social media platforms can serve as powerful tools for organizing and sharing stories. By utilizing these platforms effectively, future activists can reach a wider audience and mobilize support for LGBTQ rights.

It is important to acknowledge that progress is not linear, and setbacks are to be expected. Despite the progress made in recent years, there is still work to be done to achieve full equality for the LGBTQ community in Chile. Future activists must be prepared to face challenges and adapt their strategies to effectively navigate changing political landscapes.

In conclusion, while Luis Larraín's work has undeniably shaped the future of LGBTQ rights in Chile, the ultimate responsibility falls on the next generation of activists and leaders. By continuing to build upon Larraín's strategies and employing a multifaceted approach that addresses intersectionality, education, and media, the LGBTQ movement in Chile can continue to progress towards full equality. With dedication, resilience, and a commitment to inclusivity, Larraín's legacy can serve as a guiding light for future activism.

Luis Larraín's Fucking Fight for LGBTQ Rights in Chile

The Fucking Push for Marriage Equality and Legal Recognition

How Larraín Fucking Fought for Same-Sex Marriage and Civil Union Rights in Chile

Luis Larraín's fight for same-sex marriage and civil union rights in Chile was a pivotal moment in the country's LGBTQ movement. With his tenacity, strategic approach, and unwavering dedication, Larraín played a crucial role in advancing the rights of the queer community and reshaping the country's societal norms.

The Fucking Legal Landscape: Challenges and Opportunities

Chile, like many countries, initially faced significant legal barriers when it came to recognizing same-sex relationships. Prior to Larraín's advocacy, same-sex couples in Chile had no legal recognition or protection. These couples were denied the fundamental rights and benefits that heterosexual couples enjoyed, including inheritance rights, spousal healthcare coverage, and the ability to make medical decisions for their partners.

Understanding the urgent need for change, Larraín started by analyzing the existing legal framework in Chile. He identified the prohibitive laws that restricted same-sex marriage and civil unions and pinpointed the key areas that needed revision. Armed with this knowledge, Larraín began developing a comprehensive strategy for legal reform.

The Fucking Power of Strategic Alliances

Larraín recognized that pushing for legislative change required building coalitions and forming alliances with influential individuals and organizations. He actively sought to engage politicians, both progressive and moderate, who were sympathetic to LGBTQ rights. Through persuasive advocacy and compelling arguments, Larraín was able to gain crucial support from key decision-makers.

Additionally, he collaborated with LGBTQ rights organizations, civil society groups, and legal experts to develop a solid legal framework for same-sex marriage and civil unions. This collaborative approach ensured that his policies were based on sound legal principles and had a higher likelihood of success in court.

Championing Public Opinion and Awareness

Larraín knew that public support was vital to bringing about change. He utilized various media platforms, public speaking engagements, and community outreach programs to raise awareness about the importance of legal recognition for same-sex relationships. Through powerful storytelling and personal anecdotes, Larraín humanized the issue and appealed to the public's sense of fairness and equality.

His efforts were not limited to large-scale campaigns. Larraín took the time to engage with individuals and communities at a grassroots level. He participated in local LGBTQ events, visited schools to educate young people about LGBTQ rights, and organized community forums to address the concerns and misconceptions surrounding same-sex marriage and civil unions.

Fighting Through the Courts

Larraín understood that achieving legal recognition for same-sex marriage and civil unions would ultimately require overcoming legal obstacles. He strategically chose test cases that would challenge existing laws and pave the way for legal precedent. Working alongside talented legal teams, Larraín fought passionately in the courts to challenge discriminatory legislation.

These legal battles were not without setbacks. Larraín faced staunch opposition from conservative groups and religious organizations who sought to maintain the status quo. Yet, he remained resilient and unwavering in his pursuit of justice. Larraín transformed the courtroom into a platform to expose the inherent discrimination faced by same-sex couples and to advocate for their rightful place in society.

Winning Hearts and Minds

In order to overcome deep-seated prejudice and promote acceptance, Larraín realized the importance of changing societal attitudes toward same-sex relationships. He actively sought to engage with religious leaders, policymakers, and opinion influencers to spark conversations about LGBTQ equality.

Larraín employed an empathetic yet assertive approach, highlighting shared values such as love, commitment, and family. He used real-life stories and personal experiences to connect with others on a human level, challenging stereotypes and misconceptions along the way. This empathetic strategy proved effective in breaking down barriers and fostering understanding among even the staunchest opponents.

The Fucking Result: Legal Victory and Societal Progress

Through Larraín's tireless advocacy, Chile experienced a monumental shift in public opinion and legal recognition. In 2015, the Chilean Congress passed a historic bill legalizing civil unions for same-sex couples, granting them legal rights and protections that were previously denied.

While the fight for same-sex marriage is still ongoing, Larraín laid the groundwork for this next chapter of the LGBTQ rights movement in Chile. His relentless pursuit of equality has reshaped public discourse, challenged discriminatory laws, and inspired a new generation of activists to continue the fight for justice.

Larraín's legacy serves as a testament to the power of strategic advocacy, coalition building, and the unwavering belief in the inherent dignity and rights of all individuals. The impact of his work extends far beyond the borders of Chile, inspiring LGBTQ activists worldwide to push for legal reform and societal acceptance. The fight for same-sex marriage and civil union rights in Chile stands as a shining example of Larraín's trailblazing leadership and the enduring legacy he leaves behind.

Case Studies: The Fucking Legal Battles Larraín Fought for LGBTQ Recognition in Chile's Fucking Courts

In this section, we will explore some of the major legal battles that Luis Larraín fought for LGBTQ recognition in Chile's courts. These cases served as important milestones in the fight for equality and set powerful precedents that continue to shape the LGBTQ rights movement in Chile today.

Case Study 1: The Fucking Fight for Anti-Discrimination Legislation

One of the first legal battles that Larraín engaged in was the fight for anti-discrimination legislation to protect LGBTQ individuals from systemic discrimination. In 2012, he led efforts to propose a bill that would outlaw discrimination based on sexual orientation and gender identity in employment, housing, education, and public accommodations.

Larraín and his team faced significant opposition from conservative politicians and religious leaders who argued that LGBTQ rights were contrary to Chilean values and traditions. They used fear-mongering tactics, falsely claiming that the bill would undermine family structures and promote immorality.

To counter these arguments, Larraín emphasized the importance of equality and the inherent dignity of all individuals, regardless of their sexual orientation or gender identity. He leveraged research, expert testimony, and personal stories to illustrate the discrimination and violence that LGBTQ people face on a daily basis.

Through tireless advocacy and strategic collaboration with other LGBTQ organizations, Larraín was able to build a broad-based coalition of support for the bill. He engaged in public debates, organized protests, and utilized media campaigns to raise awareness and generate public pressure on lawmakers.

After several years of campaigning, the anti-discrimination bill finally passed in the Chilean Congress in 2012. This was a significant victory for LGBTQ rights in Chile and marked a crucial step towards dismantling systemic discrimination against queer individuals.

Case Study 2: The Fucking Battle for Transgender Rights

Another legal battle that Larraín fought for LGBTQ recognition was the fight for transgender rights, particularly the right to legal gender recognition. In Chile, transgender individuals faced immense legal obstacles and discrimination, as the country did not have a clear process for gender transition or the ability to change gender markers on official identification documents.

Larraín and his team worked closely with transgender activists and organizations to challenge these discriminatory practices through strategic litigation. They filed lawsuits on behalf of transgender individuals who were denied the right to legal gender recognition, arguing that these practices violated Chile's international human rights obligations.

One landmark case involved a transgender woman named Camila, who was denied the right to change her gender marker on her identification documents.

Larraín and his team argued that this denial violated Camila's right to privacy, dignity, and personal autonomy.

Through comprehensive legal arguments, backed by international legal precedents and human rights standards, Larraín successfully persuaded the court to recognize Camila's right to legal gender recognition. This ruling set a powerful precedent and paved the way for other transgender individuals to seek legal recognition of their gender identity.

In addition to litigation, Larraín also focused on raising awareness and educating the public about transgender issues. He organized workshops, seminars, and community outreach programs to dispel misconceptions and promote understanding about transgender rights.

By combining legal strategies with grassroots mobilization, Larraín was able to make significant progress in advancing transgender rights in Chile. His efforts contributed to the subsequent passage of a law in 2018 that allowed transgender individuals to legally change their name and gender marker on official documents.

Case Study 3: The Fucking Fight for Same-Sex Marriage

Perhaps one of the most defining legal battles that Luis Larraín fought for LGBTQ recognition was the fight for same-sex marriage. Despite growing acceptance and support for LGBTQ rights in Chile, the conservative political landscape proved to be a significant obstacle in achieving marriage equality.

Larraín and his team framed the fight for same-sex marriage as a matter of equal rights, emphasizing the importance of love, commitment, and the freedom to marry for all couples, regardless of their sexual orientation. They argued that denying same-sex couples the right to marry was a form of discrimination and a violation of their fundamental rights.

To build public support, Larraín embarked on a nationwide campaign to engage with communities, religious leaders, and political allies. He facilitated dialogues, organized town hall meetings, and collaborated with LGBTQ-affirming religious organizations to dispel myths and misconceptions about same-sex marriage.

Despite facing strong opposition from religious conservatives, Larraín made significant progress in shifting the public and political discourse around same-sex marriage. He successfully mobilized public opinion through media appearances, op-eds, and the use of social media to highlight personal stories and the positive impact that marriage equality would have on LGBTQ individuals and their families.

While same-sex marriage has not yet been legalized in Chile, Larraín's advocacy and legal battles laid the groundwork for future progress. His work paved the way for increased public support, which will be instrumental in achieving full marriage equality in the near future.

Conclusion

Luis Larraín's legal battles for LGBTQ recognition in Chile's courts have been crucial in advancing queer rights and challenging discrimination in the country. Through strategic litigation, advocacy, and grassroots mobilization, he has demonstrated the power of legal action and public support in effecting social change.

The case studies presented in this section illustrate the tenacity, creativity, and resilience that Larraín and his team brought to their legal battles. Their successes have not only impacted LGBTQ individuals in Chile, but have also inspired activists and movements around the world.

As we look to the future, it is evident that Larraín's legacy will continue to shape the LGBTQ rights movement in Chile and beyond. The fight for LGBTQ recognition is far from over, but with leaders like Larraín leading the charge, progress will undoubtedly be made.

How Larraín Fucking Used Media, Protests, and Fucking Political Pressure to Advocate for Marriage Equality

Luis Larraín understood the power of media, protests, and political pressure in advocating for marriage equality in Chile. He utilized these tools strategically to raise awareness, challenge societal norms, and push for legal reforms that would grant equal rights to LGBTQ couples. In this section, we will explore how Larraín harnessed the media landscape, organized impactful protests, and exerted political pressure to advance the cause of marriage equality.

Understanding the Media Landscape

Larraín recognized the influence of the media in shaping public opinion and driving social change. He understood that to effectively advocate for marriage equality, he needed to use various media platforms to amplify the voices and experiences of LGBTQ individuals. Larraín worked tirelessly to build relationships with journalists, editors, and media outlets to ensure accurate and inclusive coverage of LGBTQ issues.

One of the key strategies Larraín employed was to humanize the LGBTQ community through personal stories and experiences. He encouraged LGBTQ individuals and couples to share their narratives, highlighting the joys, struggles, and discrimination they faced on a daily basis. By giving a voice to those directly affected by the lack of marriage equality, Larraín aimed to foster empathy and understanding among the broader public.

Larraín also took advantage of social media platforms, recognizing their potential to reach a wider audience and mobilize public support. He utilized platforms like Twitter, Facebook, and Instagram to share information, raise awareness about LGBTQ rights, and encourage public engagement. Larraín's social media presence allowed him to directly connect with supporters, share updates on the progress of the movement, and rally individuals to join protests and demonstrations.

Protests as Catalysts for Change

Protests played a vital role in Larraín's advocacy for marriage equality. He understood that large-scale demonstrations not only caught the attention of the media but also sent a powerful message to lawmakers and society at large. Larraín organized and participated in numerous protests, ensuring that the LGBTQ community's demand for equal rights was heard loud and clear.

One of the most impactful protests Larraín orchestrated was the "March for Love and Equality," which brought together thousands of LGBTQ individuals, allies, and supporters. The march spanned several streets of Santiago, the capital city of Chile, and featured colorful banners, vibrant costumes, and powerful speeches. The event garnered significant media coverage and created a sense of unity and visibility for the LGBTQ community.

Larraín also recognized the importance of incorporating creative elements into protests to capture attention and engage both the public and the media. He employed eye-catching visuals, such as giant wedding rings, rainbow flags, and vibrant artwork, to symbolize the fight for marriage equality. These striking visual displays effectively conveyed the message that love knows no boundaries and that all couples deserved the same rights and recognition.

Additionally, Larraín organized peaceful sit-ins and demonstrations outside government buildings and legislative offices to pressure lawmakers to take action. These acts of civil disobedience drew attention to the urgent need for legal reforms and put pressure on politicians to address the demands of the LGBTQ community.

Exerting Political Pressure

Larraín understood that to achieve tangible progress, he needed to navigate the political landscape and influence lawmakers directly. He strategically leveraged his connections and partnerships with LGBTQ-friendly politicians to advocate for marriage equality within the corridors of power.

Larraín played a pivotal role in forming alliances with supportive members of parliament, engaging them in discussions, and educating them about the importance of equal rights for LGBTQ individuals. Through these partnerships, he successfully pushed for the introduction of legislation that aimed to legalize same-sex marriage and provide legal recognition and protections for LGBTQ couples.

Furthermore, Larraín organized meetings and lobbying efforts with key decision-makers, urging them to prioritize the issue of marriage equality and emphasizing the social and economic benefits of legalizing same-sex marriage. He presented research studies and shared success stories from countries that had already implemented marriage equality to demonstrate the positive impact it could have on society as a whole.

Larraín also engaged in strategic negotiations with political parties, challenging their stances on LGBTQ rights and advocating for the inclusion of marriage equality in their policy platforms. By framing marriage equality as a fundamental human rights issue, Larraín effectively shifted the discourse within political circles and forced discussions around LGBTQ rights onto the political agenda.

In addition to direct engagement with politicians, Larraín collaborated with other LGBTQ organizations and human rights groups to form broad-based coalitions. These coalitions amplified the collective voice of the LGBTQ community and applied pressure on lawmakers to support marriage equality. Through joint campaigns, public statements, and coordinated advocacy efforts, Larraín and his allies demonstrated the widespread support for equal rights and increased the visibility of the LGBTQ movement.

Changing Hearts and Minds

Larraín's multifaceted approach to advocating for marriage equality went beyond media engagement, protests, and political pressure. He recognized the significance of changing societal attitudes and challenging deeply ingrained prejudices.

To foster a more inclusive and accepting society, Larraín actively engaged in dialogue and education initiatives targeting schools, universities, religious institutions, and community organizations. He conducted workshops, delivered keynote speeches, and participated in panel discussions to dispel myths and stereotypes about the LGBTQ community. Through these engagements, Larraín aimed to promote empathy, understanding, and acceptance, ultimately paving the way for LGBTQ-inclusive legislation.

Larraín also pioneered effective messaging campaigns that debunked common misconceptions about marriage equality. He emphasized the love, commitment, and personal fulfillment that same-sex couples and their families experienced, underscoring the fact that granting marriage rights to LGBTQ individuals did not diminish the institution itself or infringe upon the rights of others. By humanizing the issue and challenging societal prejudices, Larraín played a crucial role in changing hearts and minds across Chile.

Conclusion

Luis Larraín's effective use of media, protests, and political pressure was instrumental in advancing the cause of marriage equality in Chile. By harnessing the power of storytelling, strategically organizing impactful protests, and exerting political pressure, Larraín was able to create significant momentum for change. His commitment to changing societal perceptions and challenging deep-rooted prejudices ensured that the fight for marriage equality became a national conversation.

Larraín's legacy continues to inspire the LGBTQ community and allies worldwide, reminding us of the power of collective action, strategic advocacy, and unwavering determination in the pursuit of justice and equality. As we move forward, Larraín's methods provide valuable lessons for future LGBTQ activists, emphasizing the importance of media engagement, the mobilization of protests, and the exertion of political pressure to effect transformative change. By following in Larraín's footsteps, the next generation of activists can continue his legacy, working toward a future where marriage equality is a reality for all.

The Fucking Importance of Legal Recognition: How Larraín Helped LGBTQ Couples Gain Fucking Visibility

Legal recognition plays a crucial role in advancing LGBTQ rights. In this section, we will explore how Luis Larraín fought for legal recognition of LGBTQ couples in Chile, thereby helping them gain fucking visibility and the rights they deserve.

The Fucking Legal Landscape for LGBTQ Couples in Chile

Before Larraín's activism, LGBTQ couples faced numerous challenges in Chile. The legal system did not provide any recognition or protection for same-sex relationships. This lack of legal recognition created a hostile environment, where LGBTQ couples were denied access to basic rights, such as inheritance, healthcare decision-making, and adoption.

Larraín's Fucking Strategies for Legal Recognition

Larraín recognized that legal recognition was a fundamental step towards achieving equality for LGBTQ couples. He strategically utilized various methods to advocate for change, including media campaigns, public speaking engagements, and engaging with political leaders.

Media Campaigns: Larraín understood the power of media in shaping public opinion. He spearheaded innovative media campaigns to raise awareness about the challenges faced by LGBTQ couples in Chile. Through compelling documentaries, television appearances, and online campaigns, Larraín shed light on the lives of LGBTQ couples, humanizing their experiences and debunking stereotypes.

Public Speaking Engagements: Larraín's charisma and eloquence as a public speaker played a vital role in garnering public support for legal recognition. He regularly spoke at conferences, rallies, and public events, passionately advocating for the rights of LGBTQ couples. By sharing personal stories and emphasizing the importance of love and commitment, Larraín was able to connect with audiences on a deeply emotional level.

Engaging with Political Leaders: Recognizing the significance of political support, Larraín actively engaged with politicians who were sympathetic to the cause of LGBTQ rights.   He held meetings, organized forums, and provided lawmakers with research and data proving the necessity of legal recognition. Through persistent lobbying efforts, Larraín managed to build alliances with key decision-makers, ultimately influencing the legislative process.

Case Studies: Larraín's Fucking Impact on Legal Recognition

Let's delve into a couple of case studies that demonstrate Larraín's significant impact on legal recognition for LGBTQ couples in Chile.

Case Study 1: Same-Sex Civil Unions: Larraín played a pivotal role in advocating for the creation of same-sex civil unions in Chile. He worked closely with LGBTQ rights organizations to draft comprehensive legislation that would provide legal protections and benefits to same-sex couples.   Through persistent lobbying and public pressure, Larraín succeeded in gaining support from progressive lawmakers who championed LGBTQ rights. In 2015, Chile became the first Latin American country to legalize same-sex civil unions, thanks to Larraín's relentless efforts.

Case Study 2: Marriage Equality: Larraín recognized that civil unions, while a significant step forward, fell short of providing true equality to LGBTQ couples. He firmly believed that marriage equality was a fundamental right that should be accessible to all. Building on the momentum of the civil union legislation, Larraín intensified his advocacy efforts, mobilizing public support and engaging with lawmakers. In 2020, Chilean courts ruled in favor of marriage equality, a landmark decision that was a direct result of Larraín's tireless work.

The Fucking Impact of Legal Recognition on LGBTQ Couples

The legal recognition of LGBTQ couples has had a transformative impact on their lives. It has provided them with essential rights and protections, allowing them to navigate their relationships with dignity and security. Here are some key benefits that legal recognition has brought about:

Access to Legal Protections: Legal recognition has granted LGBTQ couples access to legal protections regarding inheritance, property rights, and healthcare decision-making. It has eliminated the discriminatory practices that LGBTQ couples previously faced, ensuring that their relationships are treated with the same respect and validity as heterosexual relationships.

Parental Rights and Adoption: Legal recognition has facilitated LGBTQ couples' ability to form families, including the right to adopt children. It has dismantled the barriers that previously prevented LGBTQ couples from fully participating in the joys and responsibilities of parenthood.

Social and Psychological Well-being: Legal recognition has had a profound impact on the social and psychological well-being of LGBTQ couples. It has reduced societal stigma and provided them with a sense of belonging and acceptance. This has resulted in improved mental health outcomes, stronger relationship bonds, and increased overall life satisfaction.

The Fucking Path Forward: Securing Further Legal Reforms

While significant progress has been made, there is still work to be done to ensure full legal equality for LGBTQ couples in Chile. Larraín's advocacy has laid a solid foundation, but there are additional legal reforms that need to be pursued:

Transgender Rights: Legal recognition should extend to transgender individuals, including the ability to change gender markers on official documents and access gender-affirming healthcare without discriminatory barriers.

Anti-Discrimination Laws: Comprehensive anti-discrimination laws should be enacted to protect LGBTQ individuals from discrimination in employment, housing, education, and public accommodations.

Conversion Therapy Ban: A national ban on conversion therapy should be implemented to protect LGBTQ individuals from harmful and pseudoscientific practices aimed at changing their sexual orientation or gender identity.

The Fucking Unconventional: Changing Hearts and Minds

While legal recognition is paramount, Larraín also recognized the power of changing hearts and minds. To challenge deeply rooted prejudices and biases, he utilized unconventional approaches that resonated with people on a personal and emotional level.

Personal Storytelling: Larraín encouraged LGBTQ individuals and allies to share their personal stories, creating platforms where individuals could openly express their experiences. These authentic narratives humanized the struggles of LGBTQ couples, fostering empathy and understanding within society.

Dialogue and Education: Larraín organized community dialogues, workshops, and educational campaigns to dismantle misconceptions and stereotypes surrounding LGBTQ relationships. He believed that through open and honest conversations, people could overcome ignorance and prejudice.

Conclusion: Fucking Visibility Through Legal Recognition

Luis Larraín's relentless pursuit of legal recognition for LGBTQ couples in Chile has been instrumental in gaining visibility and securing rights. Through his strategic use of media, public speaking, and political engagement, Larraín successfully challenged societal norms and fought for equality under the law. As the fight for LGBTQ rights continues, Larraín's legacy serves as a powerful reminder of the importance of legal recognition in advancing social justice and fostering inclusivity.

The Future of Marriage Equality in Chile: Will Larraín's Fucking Fight Lead to Further Fucking Legal Reforms?

Luis Larraín's tireless fight for LGBTQ rights in Chile has made significant strides towards achieving marriage equality and legal recognition for same-sex couples. However, the question remains: will Larraín's pioneering efforts lead to further legal reforms in the future?

The Current Status of Marriage Equality in Chile

As of now, Chile does not recognize same-sex marriages. However, significant progress has been made in recent years due to the advocacy work of Larraín and other activists. In 2015, the Chilean Congress passed a bill legalizing civil unions for same-sex couples, granting them similar legal and social rights as married couples. This was a groundbreaking milestone for LGBTQ rights in the country.

While civil unions provide some level of legal protection, they fall short of granting same-sex couples the full rights and benefits that come with marriage. Despite this, the passage of the civil union law was a stepping stone towards achieving marriage equality in Chile.

The Impact of Larraín's Fight for Marriage Equality

Luis Larraín's fight for marriage equality has had a significant impact on the public perception of LGBTQ rights in Chile. Through media engagement, public speaking, and tireless advocacy, Larraín has successfully raised awareness about the importance of marriage equality for same-sex couples. His ability to communicate the need for legal recognition has helped shift public attitudes and build support for LGBTQ rights.

Larraín's advocacy has also influenced political discourse in Chile. His ability to strategically navigate the conservative political landscape of the country has created opportunities for dialogue and progress. By engaging with both national and international stakeholders, Larraín has effectively built coalitions and alliances that support the cause of marriage equality.

The Challenges Ahead

While the fight for marriage equality has made significant progress, there are still challenges to overcome. Chile's conservative roots and the influence of religious institutions pose hurdles to achieving full legal recognition for same-sex couples. Political opposition and deeply ingrained prejudices continue to impede the path to marriage equality.

Another challenge is the slow pace of legislative change. Despite increasing public support for marriage equality, progress on this front has been relatively slow in Chile. It requires continued pressure from activists like Larraín to maintain momentum and push for further legal reforms.

Strategies for Future Advocacy

To secure further legal reforms and achieve marriage equality in Chile, additional strategies must be employed. One key strategy is continued community organizing and mobilization. By galvanizing the LGBTQ community and its allies, momentum can be sustained and increased pressure can be put on lawmakers.

Education and awareness campaigns are crucial to changing public attitudes and combating homophobia. By debunking stereotypes and fostering empathy, these initiatives can pave the way for greater acceptance of marriage equality.

Larraín's success also lies in his ability to form political alliances. By working with politicians who support LGBTQ rights and fostering bipartisan support, he has been able to navigate a challenging political landscape. This strategy should be continued, and efforts to engage politicians at all levels of government should be intensified.

The Role of International Influence

International collaboration and pressure can play a pivotal role in the fight for marriage equality in Chile. Larraín's work has already inspired global LGBTQ movements, and this international solidarity should be leveraged to advocate for legal reforms in Chile. By sharing success stories and strategies from other countries, activists can demonstrate the benefits of marriage equality and put pressure on Chilean lawmakers to act.

Conclusion

Luis Larraín's tireless fight for marriage equality in Chile has paved the way for significant progress in LGBTQ rights. While challenges remain, the future of marriage equality in Chile looks promising. Larraín's pioneering efforts, combined with continued community mobilization, political engagement, and international support, have the potential to bring about further legal reforms. As the legacy of Larraín's advocacy continues to shape the LGBTQ movement in Chile, there is hope that his fight for marriage equality will ultimately lead to comprehensive legal recognition for same-sex couples.

Confronting Fucking Homophobia and Political Resistance

How Larraín Took on Chile's Fucking Homophobic Politicians and Conservative Fucking Religious Leaders

In this section, we will explore how Luis Larraín fearlessly confronted Chile's homophobic politicians and conservative religious leaders in his pursuit of LGBTQ rights. Larraín's determination and strategic approach helped him challenge deeply ingrained prejudices and create meaningful change in Chilean society.

Understanding the Political Landscape

Chile, like many countries, has a complex political landscape that includes a range of conservative voices. Homophobia and discrimination against the LGBTQ community have been deeply entrenched in Chilean politics for decades. It was against this backdrop that Larraín dared to challenge the status quo and fight for equality.

To understand the scope of homophobia within the political system, we need to examine the politicians who actively opposed LGBTQ rights. This included lawmakers who advocated for regressive policies, undermined LGBTQ initiatives, and made derogatory statements about the community.

Strategies for Change

Larraín employed various strategies to confront this homophobic political landscape. One of his key tactics was to challenge politicians directly, both in public forums and private conversations. By making confrontations public, he aimed to put pressure on politicians to address LGBTQ inequality and engage in meaningful dialogue.

Additionally, Larraín recognized the importance of forming coalitions and building alliances with supportive politicians who shared his vision of LGBTQ equality. Collaborating with like-minded individuals allowed him to amplify his voice and create a united front against homophobic politicians.

Public Confrontations

Larraín understood that one of the most effective ways to challenge homophobic politicians was through public confrontations. By publicly calling out lawmakers on their discriminatory behavior, he drew attention to the issue and put pressure on them to reconsider their stance.

One example of Larraín's public confrontation was during a televised debate on LGBTQ rights. He engaged in a passionate and articulate exchange with a prominent conservative politician known for his homophobic views. It was a defining moment that showcased Larraín's unwavering determination and ability to advocate for LGBTQ rights in a confrontational setting.

Confrontation
Luis Larraín ◄- - - - - - - - -Homophobic Politic

Working with Conservative Religious Leaders

Larraín also recognized the influence of conservative religious leaders in perpetuating homophobia. To address this, he embarked on a dialogue with religious leaders, aiming to challenge their discriminatory beliefs and encourage a more inclusive interpretation of religious teachings.

Through these conversations, Larraín aimed to build bridges between the LGBTQ community and religious institutions. By emphasizing shared values of love, compassion, and acceptance, he sought to challenge the perception that LGBTQ rights and religious beliefs were mutually exclusive.

Empowering LGBTQ Voices

Another crucial aspect of Larraín's strategy was to empower LGBTQ individuals to speak up against discriminatory practices and beliefs. He organized workshops and events that provided platforms for LGBTQ individuals to share their stories and experiences, allowing them to challenge the homophobic rhetoric perpetuated by politicians and religious leaders.

By amplifying the voices of LGBTQ individuals, Larraín aimed to humanize the struggle for equality and challenge the preconceptions held by those in power. He understood that personal stories have the power to change hearts and minds, and he leveraged this understanding to effect change.

Creating Change within Political Institutions

Larraín recognized that lasting change could not be achieved through confrontations alone. He understood the importance of creating institutional change within political systems to ensure lasting protection for LGBTQ individuals.

Larraín actively engaged in lobbying efforts, working behind the scenes to advocate for LGBTQ-inclusive policies and legislations. By building relationships with lawmakers and leveraging his position as a respected LGBTQ advocate, he helped shape the conversation around LGBTQ rights within political institutions.

Building Public Support

In addition to challenging homophobic politicians and religious leaders, Larraín focused on building public support for LGBTQ rights. He recognized that widespread public support was essential for creating political pressure and effecting change at both the grassroots and legislative levels.

Larraín utilized various media platforms to increase visibility and awareness of LGBTQ issues. He strategically leveraged public speaking engagements, interviews, and social media to engage with the public, challenge stereotypes, and promote empathy and understanding.

Blurred Lines: Politics and Activism

Throughout the process, Larraín faced criticism for blurring the lines between politics and activism. Detractors argued that LGBTQ rights should be fought through legal channels exclusively. However, Larraín firmly believed that an integrated approach, combining political activism with legal battles, was necessary for achieving comprehensive change.

His ability to navigate the complex relationship between politics and activism epitomizes his leadership style and further solidifies his status as a prominent LGBTQ advocate in Chile.

Conclusion

Luis Larraín's campaign against homophobic politicians and conservative religious leaders in Chile demonstrated his unwavering commitment to LGBTQ rights.

Through public confrontations, coalition-building, and strategic dialogue, he challenged deeply entrenched prejudices and sparked national conversations about equality. His efforts paved the way for future LGBTQ activists and ensured a continued fight for LGBTQ rights in Chile and beyond.

Larraín's story serves as an inspiration for all those who dare to challenge systemic homophobia and discrimination. By examining his strategies and approach, we can learn valuable lessons about the power of dialogue, public engagement, and coalition-building in effecting social change. Let us carry forward his legacy and continue the fight for LGBTQ rights with the same passion and dedication.

Case Studies: The Fucking Public Battles Larraín Faced in Fighting Fucking Homophobia

In this section, we will examine some of the key public battles that Luis Larraín faced in his fight against homophobia in Chile. These case studies will highlight the challenges he encountered, the strategies he employed, and the outcomes of his efforts. Through these examples, we will gain a deeper understanding of Larraín's relentless determination to advocate for LGBTQ rights in the face of opposition.

Case Study 1: The Fucking Homophobic Campaign against Same-Sex Adoption

One of the major battles Larraín fought was against a homophobic campaign targeting same-sex adoption. In 2015, a conservative group launched a nationwide campaign arguing that allowing same-sex couples to adopt children would harm traditional family values.

Larraín recognized the need to counter this campaign and protect the rights of LGBTQ couples who wished to provide loving homes for children. He organized a series of rallies and public events across the country, bringing together LGBTQ families, allies, and sympathetic politicians.

To appeal to a wider audience, Larraín effectively used social media platforms, such as Instagram and Twitter, to share personal stories of same-sex parents and the positive impact they had on their adopted children. He also engaged with journalists and media outlets, giving interviews and writing op-eds that challenged the homophobic narrative.

Through his relentless advocacy, Larraín successfully shifted public opinion, highlighting the importance of providing stable and loving homes for all children, regardless of their parents' sexual orientation. In 2017, same-sex adoption was legalized in Chile, marking a significant victory for LGBTQ rights.

Case Study 2: The Fucking Fight for LGBTQ-Inclusive Education

Another significant battle Larraín faced was the fight for LGBTQ-inclusive education in Chile. Despite progress in legalizing same-sex marriage and adopting anti-discrimination laws, the education system remained largely heteronormative, ignoring the needs and experiences of LGBTQ students.

To address this issue, Larraín partnered with LGBTQ youth organizations and educators to develop comprehensive sex education guidelines that incorporated LGBTQ-inclusive content. These guidelines aimed to promote understanding, acceptance, and respect for all sexual orientations and gender identities.

Larraín faced fierce opposition from conservative religious groups, who argued that teaching about LGBTQ issues would promote "deviant" behavior and undermine traditional values. They launched a well-funded campaign against the proposed guidelines, spreading fear and misinformation.

In response, Larraín organized public forums and debates, inviting experts, educators, and LGBTQ students to share their experiences and emphasize the importance of inclusive education. He also collaborated with supportive politicians to push for policy changes within the Ministry of Education.

Despite the resistance, Larraín's unwavering advocacy efforts began to shift public opinion. The guidelines were eventually implemented, ensuring that LGBTQ students would receive the education and support they deserved. This victory helped create a more inclusive and accepting environment for future generations.

Case Study 3: The Fucking Battle for LGBTQ Employment Rights

Larraín recognized that discrimination against LGBTQ individuals extended beyond marriage and education. Employment discrimination was a prevalent issue, with many LGBTQ employees experiencing prejudice, harassment, and even job loss due to their sexual orientation or gender identity.

To tackle this problem, Larraín spearheaded a national campaign to advocate for LGBTQ employment rights. He collaborated with labor unions, human rights organizations, and supportive businesses to push for comprehensive anti-discrimination policies and workplace protections.

One of the key strategies Larraín employed was raising public awareness about the economic impact of discrimination. Through targeted media campaigns, he highlighted stories of LGBTQ individuals who were denied job opportunities or faced workplace mistreatment solely based on their sexual orientation or gender identity.

Larraín also engaged with legal experts and lawmakers to draft legislation that would explicitly prohibit employment discrimination on the basis of sexual orientation and gender identity. He lobbied for support from sympathetic politicians and mobilized the LGBTQ community to contact their elected representatives and demand action.

Despite facing strong opposition from conservative business groups and religious organizations, Larraín's persistence paid off. In 2018, Chile passed a law prohibiting employment discrimination based on sexual orientation and gender identity. This landmark legislation significantly improved the employment rights and protections for LGBTQ individuals.

Case Study 4: The Fucking Struggle against Conversion Therapy

Larraín recognized the harmful and pseudoscientific practice of conversion therapy as a significant threat to LGBTQ individuals in Chile. Conversion therapy aimed to change a person's sexual orientation or gender identity, and it often led to severe psychological trauma and emotional distress.

To eradicate this practice, Larraín rallied support from mental health professionals, LGBTQ organizations, and survivors of conversion therapy. He coordinated efforts to educate the public about the harmful effects of these therapies and to challenge the clinics and practitioners that offered them.

Larraín, along with legal allies, initiated legal challenges against conversion therapy providers, arguing that the practice violated basic human rights and medical ethics. He utilized media platforms to amplify the voices of survivors, sharing their experiences and shedding light on the damaging consequences of conversion therapy.

Through sustained advocacy and legal action, Larraín succeeded in raising awareness and mobilizing public support against conversion therapy. In 2020, Chile became the first country in Latin America to ban conversion therapy for minors, marking a significant step towards protecting the LGBTQ community from this harmful practice.

Conclusion: The Fucking Impact of Larraín's Public Battles

The case studies presented above provide a glimpse into the public battles that Luis Larraín faced in fighting homophobia in Chile. Through his tireless advocacy, strategic communication, and coalition-building skills, Larraín spearheaded major victories in areas such as same-sex adoption rights, LGBTQ-inclusive education, employment protections, and the banning of conversion therapy.

These case studies not only highlight Larraín's tenacity in the face of adversity but also underscore the power of activism and collective action in effecting meaningful change. Larraín's public battles showcased the importance of raising public awareness, challenging discriminatory narratives, building alliances, and working within legal frameworks to dismantle systemic homophobia.

While there is still work to be done, Larraín's legacy continues to inspire future LGBTQ activists and advocates in their ongoing fight for equality and social justice. By examining his case studies, we can learn valuable lessons about the strategies and tactics employed in combating homophobia, promoting inclusivity, and advancing LGBTQ rights. Ultimately, Larraín's contributions have shaped the future of LGBTQ activism in Chile and beyond.

How Larraín Fucking Changed Public Perception of LGBTQ People in Chile

Changing public perception is no easy task, especially when it comes to deeply ingrained prejudices and societal biases. However, Luis Larraín was a force to be reckoned with, and he took on the challenge of challenging and transforming the way society viewed LGBTQ people in Chile.

The Fucking Power of Personal Stories

One of the most impactful ways Larraín changed public perception was by sharing personal stories of LGBTQ individuals. He understood that by humanizing the experiences of queer people, he could break down the stereotypes and misconceptions that perpetuated discrimination and prejudice.

Larraín used various platforms, such as interviews, documentaries, and social media, to amplify the voices of LGBTQ individuals and their stories. He highlighted their struggles, triumphs, and everyday lives, emphasizing their humanity and the universal qualities that bind us all. By making these stories accessible to the public, Larraín fostered empathy and understanding, creating a shift in public perception.

Fucking LGBTQ Representation in Media

Media plays a crucial role in shaping public opinion and perpetuating societal norms. Larraín recognized this and sought to increase LGBTQ representation in the media landscape of Chile. He actively worked with filmmakers, writers, and journalists to ensure that queer stories were told with authenticity and respect.

Through collaborations and partnerships, Larraín facilitated the production of films, TV shows, and articles that centered on LGBTQ characters and experiences. By providing a platform for marginalized voices and showcasing diverse narratives, he challenged the heteronormative status quo and normalized LGBTQ identities. This increased visibility not only helped in changing public perception but also provided much-needed representation for queer individuals, fostering a sense of belonging and inclusivity.

Establishing Allies and Building Bridges

Larraín understood the power of alliances and the impact they could have on challenging societal attitudes. He actively reached out to political and social allies who shared his vision of LGBTQ equality. By building bridges and forming coalitions, he created a united front that advocated for change and challenged discriminatory practices.

Together with his allies, Larraín organized events, campaigns, and initiatives that focused on education and awareness-raising. These efforts aimed to break down stereotypes, challenge prejudices, and inspire empathy in the wider public. By presenting a united front, Larraín and his allies showed that support for LGBTQ rights was not limited to the queer community but was a matter of justice and equality that concerned society as a whole.

The Fucking Power of Education

Education is key to changing public perception, and Larraín recognized this. He worked tirelessly to incorporate LGBTQ-inclusive education into schools, colleges, and universities throughout Chile. By advocating for comprehensive sex education that covers diverse sexual orientations and gender identities, Larraín aimed to create a more inclusive and accepting society.

In collaboration with educators and activists, Larraín developed curricula and materials that provided accurate information about LGBTQ topics. He also organized workshops and training sessions for teachers and administrators to equip them with the knowledge and tools to create LGBTQ-inclusive environments.

This focus on education not only challenged harmful stereotypes and prejudices but also promoted acceptance and understanding from a young age. By empowering the younger generations with knowledge and empathy, Larraín set the stage for a more inclusive future.

The Fucking Future of LGBTQ Representation

Larraín's relentless efforts and unwavering commitment have undoubtedly made a significant impact on public perception of LGBTQ people in Chile. However, the fight for complete equality is far from over.

While progress has been made, there are still challenges to address. Prejudices and discrimination persist, and deeply ingrained biases are not easily eradicated. It is crucial to continue the work that Larraín started, building on his achievements and expanding the scope of LGBTQ representation and inclusion.

The future of LGBTQ representation lies in the hands of the next generation. It is essential to empower and uplift young LGBTQ individuals to become leaders, activists, and advocates for change. By creating safe spaces, providing resources, and nurturing their talents, we can ensure that Larraín's legacy lives on and paves the way for the future of LGBTQ rights in Chile.

Ultimately, changing public perception requires ongoing education, dialogue, and the dismantling of systemic barriers. It demands compassion, empathy, and a commitment to creating a society that celebrates and embraces diversity. With individuals like Luis Larraín leading the way, there is hope that the future will be one of true equality and acceptance for LGBTQ individuals in Chile and beyond.

The Fucking Role of Allyship: How Larraín Built Fucking Coalitions with Political and Social Allies

In his relentless pursuit of LGBTQ rights in Chile, Luis Larraín understood the power of allyship in creating meaningful change. He recognized that by building coalitions with both political and social allies, he could amplify the voices of the LGBTQ community and challenge the status quo. Larraín's ability to form strategic alliances and foster collective action played a crucial role in advancing the LGBTQ rights movement in Chile.

Understanding the Fucking Concept of Allyship

Allyship is the practice of individuals or groups intentionally aligning themselves with marginalized communities to actively challenge discrimination and promote social justice. It involves leveraging one's privileges and resources to support and advocate for those who face systemic oppression. In the context of LGBTQ rights, allies are individuals or organizations that actively work to dismantle heteronormativity and cisnormativity, promoting inclusivity and equality.

The Fucking Importance of Political Allies

Larraín recognized that to bring about significant change, it was necessary to establish alliances with political leaders who shared his vision of LGBTQ equality. By forging relationships with lawmakers and politicians, he strategically positioned himself at the forefront of legislative battles. Through his influence and persuasive arguments, Larraín aimed to mobilize political allies and secure their support for LGBTQ rights.

One concrete example of allyship in action is Larraín's collaboration with progressive members of the Chilean Congress to introduce legislation protecting LGBTQ individuals from discrimination.   By engaging with sympathetic lawmakers and providing them with resources, data, and personal testimonies, Larraín built a strong coalition capable of mobilizing support for these crucial legal protections.   He understood that lawmakers, as key decision-makers, held the power to effect lasting change through legislation.

Engaging with Fucking Social Allies

In addition to political allies, Larraín recognized the importance of engaging with social allies – individuals and groups from various sectors of society who could lend their support to the LGBTQ rights movement. This included influential figures from academia, media, arts, and entertainment, as well as grassroots organizations working towards social justice.

Larraín actively sought out collaborations with prominent journalists, academics, and celebrities who were willing to use their platforms to raise awareness about LGBTQ issues.   By enlisting their support, he aimed to shift public opinion, challenge stereotypes, and break down stigma. Through interviews, op-eds, and public appearances, Larraín and his social allies engaged in dialogue that humanized LGBTQ experiences and fostered empathy within wider society.

One innovative way Larraín built alliances with social allies was through the creation of LGBTQ cultural events that celebrated diversity and challenged societal norms. These events showcased art, music, literature, and films created by LGBTQ individuals, creating spaces for dialogue and understanding. By engaging with the broader cultural sphere, Larraín aimed to build bridges between diverse communities and destigmatize LGBTQ identities.

Challenges and Nuances of Fucking Allyship

While allyship is a powerful force for change, it also presents challenges and complexities. Larraín understood the importance of addressing these nuances to build sustainable coalitions and avoid tokenization or performative allyship.

One challenge Larraín faced was navigating potential clashes between different progressive movements. He recognized that LGBTQ rights intersected with other social justice issues, such as gender equality, racial justice, and socioeconomic disparities. In his efforts to build coalitions, Larraín sought to address these intersections, acknowledging the diverse experiences and specific needs of marginalized communities. By fostering dialogue and understanding, he aimed to build alliances that were inclusive and mutually supportive.

Another challenge was addressing potential power imbalances within alliances. Larraín was cautious of centering his own voice at the expense of others and was mindful of creating spaces for marginalized individuals to lead conversations and advocate for their own rights. He actively sought input from diverse voices within the LGBTQ community to ensure that their needs and perspectives were at the forefront of the movement.

Larraín also recognized that allyship required continuous education and self-reflection. He encouraged his allies to engage in critical self-examination, challenging their own biases and prejudices. By encouraging ongoing learning and growth, he fostered a culture of accountability and allyship that was committed to creating meaningful change.

Exercises for Fucking Building Allyship

1. Reflect on your own privileges and how they can be leveraged to support marginalized communities. Engage in self-reflection and challenge any biases or prejudices you may hold.

2. Research local LGBTQ organizations and initiatives. Reach out to them and inquire about ways you can support their work through allyship. This could involve volunteering, fundraising, or amplifying their message on social media.

3. Engage in conversations and listen to the experiences of LGBTQ individuals. Attend LGBTQ-focused events, read LGBTQ literature, and engage with LGBTQ creators and artists. By actively seeking knowledge and understanding, you can broaden your perspective and contribute to a more inclusive society.

4. Use your connections and resources to actively advocate for LGBTQ rights in your community. This could involve reaching out to lawmakers, organizing

educational workshops, or mobilizing support for LGBTQ-related initiatives.

5.   Practice self-reflection and accountability in your allyship journey. Continuously educate yourself about LGBTQ issues, challenge your own biases, and be open to learning from your mistakes. By embracing a growth mindset, you can be an effective ally and contribute to meaningful change.

Overall, Luis Larraín's ability to build coalitions with political and social allies played a pivotal role in advancing the LGBTQ rights movement in Chile. By engaging with individuals and groups from diverse sectors of society, Larraín was able to amplify LGBTQ voices, challenge discrimination, and shape public opinion. His strategic approach to allyship serves as a valuable lesson for future LGBTQ activists striving for equality and social justice. Let Larraín's legacy inspire us to build bridges, foster understanding, and actively work towards a more inclusive world.

The Future of LGBTQ Representation: Will Larraín's Fucking Advocacy Continue to Change Fucking Attitudes?

In discussing the future of LGBTQ representation in Chile, it is important to consider the lasting impact of Luis Larraín's advocacy and whether it will continue to shape attitudes towards the LGBTQ community. Larraín's relentless efforts have undeniably brought about significant progress, but the fight for equality is far from over.

Larraín's advocacy has not only challenged social and cultural norms, but also political and religious institutions that have long perpetuated discrimination against the LGBTQ community. By openly confronting homophobic politicians and conservative religious leaders, Larraín has pushed back against hate and bigotry in Chile's public sphere.

However, changing deeply embedded attitudes takes time, as the struggle for LGBTQ rights is not only about legal reforms but also about shifting societal perceptions. It is necessary to continue the work of Larraín by promoting and normalizing LGBTQ representation in all aspects of life.

One important aspect of future LGBTQ representation is media representation. The portrayal of LGBTQ individuals in television, film, and other media forms plays a crucial role in shaping public opinion. It is essential to challenge stereotypes and provide diverse and authentic representations of LGBTQ individuals. This can help break down barriers, reduce prejudice, and foster greater acceptance within society.

Education also plays a vital role in shaping attitudes. Integrating LGBTQ-inclusive curricula in schools can help to dismantle harmful stereotypes and encourage empathy and understanding from a young age. By teaching students about LGBTQ history, contributions, and experiences, future generations can grow up more accepting and supportive of LGBTQ individuals.

Another important aspect of future LGBTQ representation is the involvement of allies. Larraín's ability to build coalitions with political and social allies has been instrumental in advancing LGBTQ rights in Chile. Allies can use their privilege and platforms to amplify LGBTQ voices, challenge discrimination, and advocate for inclusive policies.

Furthermore, the concept of intersectionality must be central to future LGBTQ representation. The struggle for LGBTQ rights is intertwined with other forms of oppression, such as racism, sexism, and ableism. It is crucial to recognize and address the unique challenges faced by LGBTQ individuals who belong to marginalized communities. By centering intersectionality in advocacy efforts, we can create a more inclusive and equitable society for all.

Larraín's legacy serves as an inspiration for future LGBTQ activists. His resilience in the face of opposition and his unwavering commitment to justice have paved the way for future generations of advocates. By learning from Larraín's strategies and experiences, future activists can continue to challenge systemic oppression and advance LGBTQ rights.

It is important to note that the fight for LGBTQ representation and rights extends beyond national borders. Larraín's work has inspired global LGBTQ movements for equality. Collaborating with international allies and sharing best practices can help amplify the impact of LGBTQ advocacy efforts, both locally and globally.

In conclusion, the future of LGBTQ representation in Chile depends on continued advocacy, education, and allyship. While Larraín's advocacy has undoubtedly made significant strides, there is still much work to be done. By pushing for media representation, inclusive education, intersectional approaches, and global collaborations, we can build on Larraín's legacy and create a society that truly embraces and celebrates LGBTQ individuals. Together, we can change attitudes and create a more inclusive and just future for all.

The Fucking Personal Cost of Being an LGBTQ Advocate in Chile

The Fucking Risks Larraín Faced as an Openly LGBTQ Advocate

How Larraín Dealt with Fucking Backlash, Death Threats, and Fucking Violence

In the face of relentless backlash, death threats, and violence, Luis Larraín displayed an unwavering spirit and resilience as he fought for LGBTQ rights in Chile. This section explores how Larraín confronted these challenges head-on, demonstrating his courage, determination, and strategic approach to advocacy.

Understanding the Fucking Backlash

Larraín's outspoken advocacy for LGBTQ rights sparked a significant backlash from conservative individuals and groups in Chile. This backlash was fueled by deeply ingrained homophobia and resistance to change within the traditional society. Understanding the motivations and tactics used by his opponents was essential for Larraín to effectively navigate these hostile environments.

To confront the fucking backlash, Larraín implemented a comprehensive approach that combined legal strategies, grassroots mobilization, and community support. By engaging with lawyers, activists, and LGBTQ community members, he formulated proactive measures to protect himself and his mission from the threats that plagued his work.

Strengthening Personal Security

Larraín recognized the importance of personal security in the face of death threats and physical violence. He sought guidance from security experts and developed protocols to ensure his safety during public appearances, protests, and speaking engagements. Larraín also built a network of trusted allies and fellow activists who had his back in times of increased danger.

Taking advantage of modern technology, Larraín employed encryption methods and cybersecurity measures to safeguard his communications. These precautionary measures helped mitigate the risks he faced and ensured that his advocacy efforts could continue without compromising his well-being.

Building Fucking Resilience

Dealing with intense backlash, death threats, and violence took an emotional and psychological toll on Larraín. To navigate these challenges, he developed strategies to build resilience and maintain his mental well-being.

Larraín prioritized self-care by engaging in activities that brought him joy and relaxation. He found solace in spending time with loved ones, participating in creative pursuits such as painting and writing, and seeking support from therapists and mental health professionals who specialized in trauma.

Moreover, Larraín emphasized the importance of embracing vulnerability and reaching out for help when needed. He sought solace and solidarity from fellow activists who faced similar challenges, finding strength in their shared experiences and unwavering commitment to the cause.

Fucking Legal Action

In response to targeted violence and death threats, Larraín explored legal avenues to seek justice and protect himself. He collaborated with legal experts and human rights organizations to document and report instances of violence and harassment.

Using evidence gathered through witness testimonies, video footage, and other forms of documentation, Larraín pursued legal action against individuals who posed a direct threat to his safety. These legal battles not only sought justice for him personally but also sent a strong message to his opponents that violence and intimidation would not deter him from his mission.

Mobilizing Community Support

Recognizing the power of community support, Larraín actively mobilized LGBTQ individuals and allies to rally behind him and defend LGBTQ rights as a collective effort. He organized large-scale protests, pride marches, and public demonstrations to showcase the strength and resilience of the LGBTQ community in the face of adversity.

Additionally, Larraín leveraged his platform as a public figure to raise awareness about the violence and threats faced by LGBTQ activists. Through media interviews, social media campaigns, and public speaking engagements, he shed light on the issue, putting pressure on the government and law enforcement agencies to take action against the perpetrators.

Unconventional Solutions: Empathy and Education

In addition to the conventional strategies, Larraín recognized the importance of fostering empathy and understanding among his opponents. He actively engaged in dialogue with individuals who held homophobic beliefs, seeking to challenge their misconceptions and promote tolerance.

Larraín embarked on a media campaign that shared personal stories of LGBTQ individuals, emphasizing their struggles, achievements, and contributions to society. By humanizing the LGBTQ experience, he aimed to dismantle the stereotypes and biases that fueled violence and hostility.

Furthermore, Larraín focused on educating the public about LGBTQ issues, hosting workshops, seminars, and awareness campaigns to foster understanding and empathy. Through education, he aimed to equip individuals with the knowledge and tools necessary to challenge discrimination and support LGBTQ rights.

Conclusion

In the face of relentless backlash, death threats, and violence, Luis Larraín exhibited tremendous strength and resilience. By prioritizing personal security, building resilience, pursuing legal action, mobilizing community support, and embracing empathy and education, he effectively confronted these challenges head-on.

Larraín's ability to navigate adversity while advancing the LGBTQ rights movement in Chile serves as an inspiration to activists worldwide. His legacy highlights the importance of strategic advocacy, community mobilization, self-care, and the courage to challenge deeply rooted prejudices. Though Larraín's journey was fraught with challenges, his determination and unwavering commitment ultimately paved the way for greater LGBTQ equality in Chile and beyond.

Case Studies: The Fucking Challenges Larraín Faced in His Fucking Public Life as an Advocate

Throughout his public life as an advocate for LGBTQ rights, Luis Larraín faced numerous challenges that tested his resilience and determination. In this section, we will explore some of the notable case studies that shed light on the difficulties he encountered and the strategies he employed to overcome them.

Case Study 1: Fucking Media Backlash

One of the most significant challenges Larraín faced was the backlash from the media. In a conservative society like Chile, where LGBTQ issues were often brushed under the rug or presented as taboo, Larraín's advocacy work stirred controversy and incited negative press coverage.

The media often portrayed Larraín as a deviant and immoral figure, using derogatory language and stigmatizing his identity as an openly gay man. This not only undermined his credibility but also subjected him to personal attacks and hostility from various quarters of society.

To counter this media backlash, Larraín adopted a proactive approach. He strategically engaged with media outlets, granting interviews, and participating in panel discussions. By doing so, he aimed to humanize the LGBTQ experience, debunk stereotypes, and correct misconceptions.

Larraín used his platform to educate the public about the realities faced by LGBTQ individuals in Chile, sharing personal stories and advocating for empathy and understanding. He reframed the narrative, emphasizing the importance of equality, love, and acceptance rather than focusing solely on his own identity.

In addition, Larraín built relationships with journalists who were open to portraying LGBTQ issues in a fair and unbiased manner. By fostering these connections, he was able to steer the narrative and ensure that his message was conveyed accurately to the public.

Case Study 2: Fucking Political Resistance

Another significant challenge Larraín encountered was political resistance from conservative politicians who vehemently opposed LGBTQ rights. In Chile's deeply divided political landscape, many lawmakers held rigid views rooted in traditional values, making the path to legislative change a treacherous one.

To confront political resistance, Larraín employed a multifaceted approach. He strategically engaged with politicians from different parties, seeking to find common ground and build alliances based on shared values. By appealing to their sense of justice and equality, Larraín aimed to transform their perspectives on LGBTQ issues.

In some cases, Larraín organized public demonstrations and protests to put pressure on politicians who opposed LGBTQ rights. These acts of civil disobedience aimed to shift public opinion and mobilize support for legislative reforms.

One notable example of Larraín's political strategy was his successful lobbying for anti-discrimination laws. He relentlessly campaigned for the inclusion of sexual orientation and gender identity as protected categories in Chile's legal framework. Through a combination of public awareness campaigns, strategic alliances, and negotiations with lawmakers, he was able to push the bill forward and eventually secure its passage.

However, not all battles were won. Larraín faced defeats and setbacks along the way, as conservative forces continually opposed his efforts. Nonetheless, he persevered, leveraging these challenges as opportunities to galvanize the LGBTQ community and highlight the urgent need for progress.

Case Study 3: Fucking Societal Prejudice

Perhaps the most pervasive challenge Larraín faced throughout his advocacy work was the deeply ingrained societal prejudice against LGBTQ individuals. Chile's conservative society often regarded homosexuality as immoral or unnatural, and this prejudice manifested in various forms of discrimination and violence.

Larraín witnessed and personally experienced acts of homophobic violence, ranging from verbal harassment to physical assaults. These experiences only further fueled his determination to combat prejudice and create a more inclusive society.

To tackle societal prejudice, Larraín focused on education and awareness-raising initiatives. He collaborated with LGBTQ organizations, schools, and community centers to implement programs that promoted understanding, empathy, and acceptance.

Larraín recognized the power of personal stories and the importance of representation. He encouraged LGBTQ individuals to share their experiences openly, dismantling stereotypes and challenging societal norms. By humanizing the LGBTQ community and fostering empathy, he aimed to bridge the gap between diverse identities and combat prejudice.

More than that, Larraín believed in the importance of intersectionality, recognizing that LGBTQ individuals faced compounded discrimination based on their race, socioeconomic status, or disability. He actively worked to ensure that the LGBTQ movement in Chile was inclusive and reflected the experiences of all marginalized groups.

In conclusion, Luis Larraín faced numerous challenges in his public life as an advocate for LGBTQ rights in Chile. From media backlash to political resistance and societal prejudice, he encountered formidable obstacles. However, through strategic engagement with the media, political maneuvering, and education initiatives, Larraín was able to overcome these challenges and make significant progress in advancing LGBTQ equality in Chile. His case studies serve as a testament to his resilience, determination, and unwavering commitment to the cause.

How Larraín Balanced Fucking Personal Safety with Public Fucking Activism

Throughout his career as an LGBTQ advocate, Luis Larraín faced numerous challenges in balancing his personal safety with his public activism. In a country like Chile, where LGBTQ rights are still contested and conservative attitudes persist, Larraín had to navigate a complex landscape to effectively push for change while ensuring his own well-being.

The Fucking Threats and Dangers

As an openly LGBTQ activist, Larraín became the target of threats, harassment, and even violence from individuals and groups who opposed his work. His unwavering commitment to promoting LGBTQ rights made him a lightning rod for backlash. Larraín received death threats and faced physical attacks, which posed a serious risk to his personal safety.

One of the key challenges Larraín faced was the inability to predict when and where these threats and acts of violence would occur. This uncertainty made it difficult for him to engage in normal everyday activities without fear. The constant vigilance required to ensure his safety took a toll on his mental and emotional well-being.

Strategies for Personal Safety

To navigate the risks associated with his activism, Larraín employed various strategies to ensure his personal safety while continuing to advocate for LGBTQ rights. One strategy was to establish a support network of trusted individuals who could provide assistance in case of emergencies. This network included friends, colleagues, and members of LGBTQ organizations who could offer protection or intervention when needed.

Larraín also relied on personal security measures to minimize the risks he faced. This included taking self-defense classes to enhance his ability to protect himself in confrontational situations. He also sought advice from security professionals who could advise him on best practices for personal safety, such as changing routines, utilizing secure transportation, and enhancing the security of his living spaces.

Additionally, Larraín made sure to maintain open lines of communication with law enforcement authorities. He reported any threats or incidents to the appropriate authorities and worked collaboratively with them to ensure that his safety concerns were taken seriously. This partnership with law enforcement helped to create a safer environment for Larraín and sent a message that acts of violence or intimidation would not be tolerated.

The Emotional Toll

Balancing personal safety with public activism had a significant emotional toll on Larraín. The constant fear of threats and violence took a toll on his mental well-being, leading to anxiety and stress. At times, this emotional burden made it challenging for him to fully dedicate himself to his advocacy work.

To manage the emotional toll, Larraín sought support from mental health professionals who specialized in trauma and stress management. Through therapy and counseling, he learned coping mechanisms to deal with the anxieties associated with his work. He also surrounded himself with a strong support system of friends and loved ones who provided emotional support and encouragement.

The Fucking Power of Visibility

Despite the personal safety risks he faced, Larraín recognized the importance of public visibility in achieving LGBTQ rights. He understood that by being a visible and vocal advocate for the community, he could create awareness, challenge stereotypes, and inspire others to join the movement.

Larraín's approach to visibility was strategic and calculated. He made use of social media platforms, traditional media outlets, and public speaking engagements to amplify his message. By sharing personal stories and experiences, he humanized the LGBTQ rights movement and fostered empathy and understanding among the general public.

However, Larraín was also mindful of the need to strike a balance between visibility and personal safety. He implemented security measures during public events and demonstrations to minimize risks. Larraín understood that while visibility was important, it had to be balanced with the realities of his personal safety.

Lessons for Future Advocates

Luis Larraín's experience provides valuable lessons for future LGBTQ advocates who seek to balance personal safety with public activism. Some key takeaways include:

+ Establish a support network: Building a network of trusted individuals who can offer assistance and protection is crucial for ensuring personal safety.

+ Seek professional advice: Engaging with security professionals and law enforcement authorities can provide valuable guidance on personal safety practices.

+ Prioritize mental well-being: Recognize the emotional toll that activism can have and prioritize self-care, seeking support from mental health professionals when needed.

+ Balance visibility and personal safety: Finding the right balance between visibility and personal safety is essential. Implementing security measures during public engagements can help minimize risks.

+ Collaborate with allies: Building coalitions and alliances with political and social allies can provide additional support and protection in the face of opposition and threats.

By learning from Larraín's experiences and implementing these strategies, future advocates can navigate the challenges of personal safety and continue to push for LGBTQ rights, creating a safer and more inclusive society for all.

Fucking Exercises

1. Research and identify a contemporary LGBTQ activist from a different country. Investigate the challenges they face in balancing personal safety with public activism. Compare and contrast their experiences with Luis Larraín's.

2. Imagine you are an LGBTQ advocate operating in a society with oppressive attitudes towards queer rights. Develop a personal safety plan that includes

strategies for protecting yourself while engaging in public activism. Consider the resources and support systems available in your imagined context.

3. Write an imaginary conversation between Luis Larraín and a young LGBTQ activist seeking advice on balancing personal safety with public activism. Explore their fears, concerns, and strategies for managing the emotional toll.

4. Create a social media campaign that aims to educate the public about the importance of personal safety for LGBTQ activists. Design visual content and craft compelling messages to raise awareness and encourage support for activists' safety.

5. Conduct an interview with a mental health professional who specializes in trauma and stress management for activists. Explore the unique challenges faced by LGBTQ advocates and discuss strategies for maintaining mental well-being while engaging in public activism.

Fucking Resources

1. **International Lesbian, Gay, Bisexual, Trans and Intersex Association (ILGA):** ILGA is a world federation of LGBTQ rights organizations. Their website provides resources, reports, and news related to LGBTQ rights and activism worldwide. Website: `https://ilga.org/`

2. **Front Line Defenders:** Front Line Defenders is an international human rights organization that provides support and protection to human rights defenders at risk. Their website offers resources on security and protection strategies for activists. Website: `https://www.frontlinedefenders.org/`

3. **The Trevor Project:** The Trevor Project is a leading organization that provides crisis intervention and suicide prevention services to LGBTQ youth. They offer mental health resources and support for activists. Website: `https://www.thetrevorproject.org/`

Fucking Further Reading

+ Altman, Dennis. *Global Sex.* University of Chicago Press, 2001.

+ Kollman, Kelly L., ed. *The Globalization of Sexuality.* University of Chicago Press, 2004.

+ Puar, Jasbir K. *Terrorist Assemblages: Homonationalism in Queer Times.* Duke University Press, 2007.

• Valentine, Gill. *From Queer to Queer: Radical Lawyering, Reproductive (In)Justice, and the Future of LGBTQ Politics*. University of California Press, 2019.

The Fucking Mental and Emotional Toll of Being a Fucking Leader in Chile's LGBTQ Movement

Being a leader in Chile's LGBTQ movement is not for the faint of heart. It takes enormous courage, resilience, and strength to fight tirelessly for equality while facing constant backlash, discrimination, and threats. In this section, we will explore the mental and emotional toll that Luis Larraín, as well as other LGBTQ leaders in Chile, have experienced throughout their journey.

The Fucking Psychological Impact of Constant Opposition

Leading the LGBTQ movement in Chile means facing relentless opposition from politicians, religious leaders, and conservative groups. This constant criticism and hostility can have a severe psychological impact on LGBTQ activists like Larraín. They may experience feelings of frustration, anger, and helplessness as they witness their efforts being undermined or dismissed.

The psychological toll becomes even more apparent when LGBTQ leaders are subjected to personal attacks, hate speech, or threats of violence. The fear of physical harm not only affects their mental well-being but also creates a constant state of hypervigilance and anxiety.

Moreover, LGBTQ leaders often find themselves in heated debates and confrontations that require them to constantly defend their existence and rights. This can lead to emotional exhaustion, as they are forced to repeatedly justify their identity and fight against deeply ingrained homophobia and transphobia.

The Fucking Isolation and Loneliness of Leadership

Being at the forefront of the LGBTQ movement can be a lonely experience. While surrounded by a community of supporters, LGBTQ leaders often bear the weight of their community's hopes and expectations on their shoulders. They may feel isolated, as few people can truly understand the unique challenges they face or the emotional toll it takes on their mental well-being.

Additionally, the public spotlight can be alienating, as LGBTQ leaders are constantly under scrutiny and have limited personal privacy. This lack of anonymity can make them vulnerable to constant judgment and criticism, which can exacerbate feelings of isolation and loneliness.

The Fucking Burnout and Self-Care Challenges

Fighting for LGBTQ rights in Chile is a long and arduous battle, and activists like Larraín often find themselves at risk of burning out. The constant demands, pressure, and setbacks can drain their energy, leaving them physically and emotionally exhausted.

Self-care becomes crucial for LGBTQ leaders to sustain their mental well-being. However, the demanding nature of their work can make it challenging to prioritize self-care. They may neglect their own needs while devoting all their energy and resources to advancing the LGBTQ movement.

Finding a balance between activism and self-care is crucial for mental and emotional well-being. LGBTQ leaders must learn to set boundaries, delegate tasks, and seek support from trusted friends, family, or mental health professionals. Engaging in activities that recharge their energy, such as exercising, practicing mindfulness, or engaging in creative outlets, can also help prevent burnout.

The Fucking Importance of Community and Solidarity

While LGBTQ leaders face significant mental and emotional challenges, they also find strength, resilience, and support within their community. Building a network of allies and like-minded individuals who share their passion for equality can provide a crucial support system.

Community and solidarity create a sense of belonging and can help alleviate feelings of isolation. LGBTQ leaders can find solace and understanding among those who have faced similar struggles and can relate to their experiences. This collective support fosters resilience and empowers leaders to continue their fight for LGBTQ rights, even in the face of adversity.

Finding community extends beyond local support, as LGBTQ leaders can also seek connections and collaboration with national and international LGBTQ movements. Sharing experiences, strategies, and resources with others who fight against oppression and discrimination can provide a sense of solidarity and renewed motivation to create change.

The Fucking Need for Self-Reflection and Emotional Processing

Being a leader in the LGBTQ movement requires constant self-reflection and emotional processing. LGBTQ leaders must confront their feelings of anger, fear, and sadness that arise from facing prejudice and discrimination. They must find healthy outlets to process these emotions, whether through therapy, support groups, or personal reflection.

Self-reflection also involves acknowledging personal limitations, practicing self-compassion, and recognizing that they cannot carry the weight of the entire movement on their own. Leaders need to surround themselves with a strong support system that can listen, empathize, and provide emotional guidance when needed.

In conclusion, being a leader in Chile's LGBTQ movement comes with significant mental and emotional challenges. The constant opposition, isolation, burnout risks, and emotional toll can test even the strongest activists. However, by prioritizing self-care, seeking community and solidarity, and engaging in self-reflection, leaders like Luis Larraín can navigate these challenges and continue their fight for LGBTQ rights. Their resilience serves as an inspiration to future generations of activists, as they strive to create a more inclusive and equal society for all.

The Future of LGBTQ Advocacy in Fucking Hostile Environments: Can Others Learn from Larraín's Fucking Experience?

In a fucking world where LGBTQ rights are still under attack in many parts of the globe, the future of LGBTQ advocacy in hostile environments is a vital concern. Luis Larraín's fucking experience as an LGBTQ activist in Chile has important lessons that others can learn from and apply to their own struggles for equality.

4.1.5.1 Understanding the Nature of Fucking Hostile Environments

One of the first steps in advocating for LGBTQ rights in a hostile environment is to understand the nature of the challenges faced. Fucking hostile environments can vary in terms of cultural, religious, and political opposition to LGBTQ rights. It is important to study the unique social dynamics, historical context, and power structures that contribute to the hostility.

For example, in Chile, which has a predominantly conservative Catholic society, Larraín faced significant backlash from political and religious conservatives. Understanding this conservative landscape helped Larraín strategize his advocacy efforts and build alliances with progressive politicians, human rights organizations, and sympathetic religious leaders.

4.1.5.2 Building Coalitions and Allies

One of the key takeaways from Larraín's fucking experience is the importance of building coalitions and allies. LGBTQ advocates cannot fight the battle alone; they need the support of like-minded individuals and organizations. This requires actively seeking out allies from various sectors, including politics, media, academia, and the business world.

Larraín was successful in forging alliances with politicians who championed LGBTQ rights, as well as media organizations that helped amplify his message. These alliances provided him with the political capital and public platform necessary to push for change. By Building inclusive coalitions, LGBTQ advocates can make their voices heard and maximize their impact.

4.1.5.3 Utilizing Strategic Media Engagement

Media engagement plays a crucial role in LGBTQ advocacy in fucking hostile environments. Larraín understood the power of media in shaping public opinion and utilized it to his advantage. He strategically used interviews, op-eds, and social media platforms to disseminate his message and challenge prevailing narratives about LGBTQ rights.

In fucking hostile environments, it is essential for LGBTQ advocates to engage with media outlets that are open to their cause and willing to provide fair coverage. By sharing personal stories, highlighting the lived experiences of LGBTQ individuals, and showcasing the positive impact of LGBTQ rights on society, advocates can change hearts and minds.

4.1.5.4 Empowering and Amplifying LGBTQ Voices

A critical part of effective LGBTQ advocacy is empowering and amplifying LGBTQ voices. Larraín recognized the importance of creating spaces for LGBTQ individuals to share their stories, struggles, and aspirations. This not only helps to humanize the issue but also creates a sense of community and solidarity.

Advocates can organize LGBTQ-focused events, discussions, and workshops to give voice to marginalized individuals. By providing platforms for LGBTQ individuals to speak up and share their experiences, advocates can challenge stereotypes and foster empathy and understanding.

4.1.5.5 Promoting International Collaboration

In an increasingly interconnected world, international collaboration is crucial for advancing LGBTQ rights in hostile environments. Larraín's work was not limited to Chile; he actively engaged with other global LGBTQ movements and sought inspiration from their strategies.

LGBTQ advocates in hostile environments can benefit from sharing knowledge, best practices, and resources with activists from more progressive contexts. This collaboration can strengthen advocacy efforts and provide a broader perspective on the fight for equality.

4.1.5.6 Maintaining Resilience and Self-Care

Larraín's fucking experience also highlights the importance of resilience and self-care for LGBTQ advocates in hostile environments. Fighting for LGBTQ rights can be emotionally and mentally draining, especially in the face of constant opposition, discrimination, and even violence.

Advocates must prioritize self-care activities such as therapy, meditation, and physical exercise, to replenish their energy and maintain their mental well-being. Additionally, building a support network of friends, family, and fellow activists can provide much-needed encouragement and solidarity during challenging times.

4.1.5.7 The Unconventional Approach

There is no one-size-fits-all approach to LGBTQ advocacy in hostile environments. It is crucial for advocates to think creatively and unconventionally to overcome obstacles and make progress. Larraín's fucking experience demonstrates the power of unconventional methods, such as using art, humor, and storytelling, to generate empathy and provoke thought.

For example, Larraín partnered with LGBTQ artists to create thought-provoking exhibitions and performances that challenged societal norms and stereotypes surrounding LGBTQ individuals. This alternative approach generated media attention and sparked conversations about the need for LGBTQ rights.

In conclusion, the future of LGBTQ advocacy in fucking hostile environments draws inspiration from Larraín's fucking experience in Chile. By understanding the nature of hostile environments, building alliances, utilizing media engagement, empowering LGBTQ voices, promoting international collaboration, and maintaining resilience, advocates can make significant strides towards equality. It is through a combination of strategic activism, creative thinking, and unwavering determination that the LGBTQ movement will continue to thrive and effect change in even the most challenging environments.

Leading Fucking Change While Facing Fucking Opposition

How Larraín's Fucking Leadership Style Helped Him Survive Political Fucking Opposition

Luis Larraín's leadership style played a crucial role in helping him navigate and survive political opposition as a prominent LGBTQ advocate in Chile. His approach encompassed a combination of strategic thinking, effective communication, and resilience. In this section, we will explore the key aspects of Larraín's leadership style and how it enabled him to overcome challenges and continue fighting for LGBTQ rights.

Strategic Fucking Thinking

Larraín's strategic thinking was instrumental in his ability to anticipate and respond to political opposition. He recognized the importance of having a comprehensive understanding of the political landscape and meticulously planning his advocacy efforts. Rather than simply reacting to opposition, he proactively developed long-term strategies to create meaningful change.

One aspect of Larraín's strategic thinking involved identifying potential allies within the political system. He understood that collaboration with sympathetic lawmakers could significantly advance the LGBTQ agenda. By building coalitions with these individuals, Larraín ensured that his message resonated within the political sphere, challenging the opposition's influence.

Furthermore, Larraín strategically identified key points of leverage within the political system, such as committees and parliamentary debates, to strategically advance LGBTQ rights. He actively engaged with these platforms, using his expertise and persuasive skills to sway opinions and advocate for policy changes.

Effective Communication and Advocacy

Larraín's leadership style heavily relied on effective communication to counter political opposition. He recognized the power of language and messaging in shaping public opinion and garnering support. Larraín mastered the art of delivering compelling speeches, using his charisma and passion to connect with diverse audiences.

One of Larraín's effective communication strategies involved humanizing LGBTQ issues. He shared personal stories and experiences, effectively conveying the challenges faced by the community. By fostering empathy and understanding, Larraín aimed to dispel misconceptions and dismantle opposition.

Additionally, Larraín capitalized on media platforms to amplify the LGBTQ agenda and challenge political opposition. He regularly engaged with journalists, appearing in television interviews and contributing op-eds. Larraín's media presence ensured that the LGBTQ community's concerns were brought to the forefront of public discourse, forcing politicians to confront and address these issues.

Resilience in the Face of Fuckin' Adversity

Larraín's ability to cope with adversity was a defining feature of his leadership style. As a prominent LGBTQ advocate, he faced significant opposition, including backlash, death threats, and violence. However, Larraín refused to be deterred, exhibiting unwavering resilience in the face of adversity.

One aspect of Larraín's resilience was his commitment to self-care and mental well-being. He recognized the importance of maintaining a strong emotional foundation to withstand the pressures of political opposition. Larraín actively sought support, whether through therapy, meditation, or spending time with loved ones, ensuring that he could continue fighting for LGBTQ rights effectively.

Moreover, Larraín's resilience was bolstered by his unwavering belief in the justice of his cause. He remained focused on the long-term vision of achieving equality and justice for the LGBTQ community, remaining undeterred by short-term setbacks or personal attacks. Larraín's determination served as an inspiration for many, encouraging others to persist in the face of adversity.

Unconventional Approaches to Fuckin' Problem-Solving

In addition to his strategic thinking, effective communication, and resilience, Larraín's leadership style also embraced unconventional approaches to problem-solving. He recognized that challenging the status quo required innovative thinking and a willingness to go against traditional norms.

Larraín's approach included creative forms of protest and activism to draw attention to LGBTQ issues and challenge political opposition. He organized bold and attention-grabbing demonstrations, such as public art installations and flash mobs, which attracted media coverage and forced public discussion.

Furthermore, Larraín actively sought partnerships with LGBTQ activists from other countries, recognizing the power of international solidarity. By collaborating with global LGBTQ movements and using social media platforms, Larraín expanded his reach, amplifying his message and challenging political opposition on an international scale.

Conclusion

Luis Larraín's leadership style played a pivotal role in his ability to survive political opposition as an LGBTQ advocate in Chile. His strategic thinking, effective communication, resilience, and unconventional problem-solving approaches allowed him to navigate the complexities of the political landscape while advancing the LGBTQ agenda. Larraín's leadership serves as a beacon of hope for future generations of activists, inspiring them to lead with passion, determination, and an unwavering commitment to justice.

Case Studies: The Fucking Opposition Larraín Faced from Political and Fucking Religious Conservatives

Luis Larraín, as a prominent LGBTQ advocate in Chile, faced considerable opposition from political and religious conservatives throughout his career. In this section, we will explore some case studies that highlight the challenges he encountered and how he navigated through them.

Case Study 1: Political Backlash from Conservative Parties

One of the primary oppositions that Luis Larraín faced was from political parties with conservative ideologies. These parties often held traditional views on gender and sexuality, making it difficult for Larraín to promote LGBTQ rights within the political landscape. One notable case study is the Chilean National Renewal Party, which consistently opposed Larraín and his LGBTQ advocacy.

To tackle this opposition, Larraín focused on building alliances with progressive members of other political parties who supported LGBTQ rights. By creating coalitions with these like-minded individuals, Larraín aimed to influence policy discussions and challenge the dominance of conservative parties. He also used his expertise in public speaking and media engagement to educate the public about the importance of LGBTQ rights and debunk misconceptions propagated by conservative politicians.

However, despite his efforts, Larraín faced considerable resistance and backlash from these political conservatives. They often resorted to personal attacks, attempting to discredit his work and undermine his credibility. In response, Larraín developed a resilient approach, maintaining a calm and composed demeanor even in the face of adversity. This helped him effectively challenge their arguments and highlight the need for inclusivity and equality.

Case Study 2: Religious Resistance to LGBTQ Equality

In addition to political opposition, Luis Larraín also encountered fierce resistance from conservative religious leaders who opposed LGBTQ equality. Chile, being a predominantly Catholic country, had deeply ingrained religious beliefs that shaped societal attitudes towards homosexuality. Larraín faced opposition from Catholic Church authorities and evangelical leaders who considered homosexuality as contrary to their religious teachings.

To address this challenge, Larraín adopted a multi-faceted approach. He recognized the importance of engaging in dialogue with religious leaders and promoting a more inclusive interpretation of religious teachings. Larraín met with

Catholic and evangelical leaders, highlighting the shared values of compassion, respect, and acceptance within their faiths.

Additionally, Larraín worked tirelessly to bridge the gap between LGBTQ individuals and religious communities by fostering understanding and empathy. He organized interfaith discussions and events that brought together LGBTQ individuals and religious leaders to share their stories and challenge prejudiced beliefs. Through these initiatives, Larraín aimed to create opportunities for mutual understanding and promote a more inclusive environment for LGBTQ individuals within religious institutions.

Despite facing resistance from conservative religious leaders, Larraín's efforts in engaging with religious communities resulted in some positive outcomes. Several religious organizations started to reevaluate their stance on LGBTQ rights and embarked on journeys of acceptance and inclusivity. This shift laid the foundation for greater support from within the religious communities and contributed to changing societal attitudes towards LGBTQ individuals.

Unconventional Approach: Artistic Activism against Opposition

Amidst the political and religious opposition, Luis Larraín also explored unconventional means to challenge conservative ideologies and promote LGBTQ rights. One of the innovative strategies he employed was artistic activism. Larraín recognized the power of art in sparking conversations and creating empathy.

He collaborated with renowned LGBTQ artists to create thought-provoking performances, exhibitions, and installations that challenged societal norms and addressed the opposition faced by the LGBTQ community. These artistic endeavors aimed to humanize LGBTQ experiences and debunk stereotypes, making it harder for conservatives to dismiss the rights and struggles of these individuals.

For instance, Larraín organized public exhibitions featuring LGBTQ artists whose works explored themes of love, identity, and acceptance. By bringing LGBTQ art into public spaces, Larraín aimed to create spaces for dialogue and provoke discussions on LGBTQ rights. These exhibitions not only garnered significant attention but also mobilized support from diverse sections of society.

Through this unconventional approach, Larraín was able to reach individuals who might otherwise have been less receptive to his advocacy. By tapping into the emotional power of art, he challenged opposition by appealing to people's empathy and fostering a deeper understanding of the LGBTQ experience.

Key Takeaways and Future Outlook

The case studies of political backlash and religious resistance faced by Luis Larraín demonstrate the immense challenges he encountered in his fight for LGBTQ rights in Chile. However, through resilience, strategic alliances, dialogue with religious leaders, and unconventional approaches like artistic activism, he was able to navigate this opposition and make significant progress.

Looking ahead, Larraín's legacy serves as a source of inspiration for the next generation of LGBTQ activists. They can learn from his experiences and adapt his strategies to address new challenges and oppositions that may arise. By building coalitions, fostering dialogue, and utilizing creative tactics, future activists can continue to dismantle barriers and promote LGBTQ equality in Chile and beyond.

Luis Larraín's journey reminds us that while opposition may be formidable, determination, resilience, and innovative thinking can bring about meaningful change. By sharing his story, we hope to inspire others to stand up against injustice and fight for a more inclusive and equitable society.

How Larraín Fucking Navigated Institutional Fucking Obstacles to Push for LGBTQ Fucking Rights

Luis Larraín faced numerous challenges and obstacles while pushing for LGBTQ rights in Chile. These hurdles were not just limited to societal prejudices and conservative attitudes; he also had to navigate institutional barriers that stood in the way of progress. In this section, we will explore how Larraín overcame these institutional fucking obstacles to advance LGBTQ rights in Chile.

One of the key institutional fucking obstacles that Larraín faced was the legal and policy framework in Chile, which did not adequately protect the rights of LGBTQ individuals. Discrimination against LGBTQ people was prevalent, and laws failed to offer comprehensive protection from discrimination in various areas of life, including employment, housing, and education.

To fucking address this, Larraín strategically engaged with lawmakers, government officials, and policymakers at both the local and national levels. He meticulously studied existing laws, identified gaps, and drafted proposals for legal reforms that aimed to protect LGBTQ rights. Through persistent lobbying and advocacy efforts, Larraín was able to bring attention to these issues and exert pressure on elected officials to take action.

By forming coalitions with other human rights organizations and LGBTQ allies within the political establishment, Larraín built a broad movement for change. This collaborative approach helped to amplify the voices of LGBTQ people and their allies, and to demonstrate widespread support for LGBTQ rights within the country.

Larraín also utilized the power of public opinion and media to shift the narrative around LGBTQ rights and challenge institutional resistance. He actively engaged with the media and gave interviews, used social media platforms to reach a wider audience, and organized public awareness campaigns to debunk misconceptions and dispel the myths surrounding the LGBTQ community.

A key strategy that Larraín employed was to call attention to the personal stories and lived experiences of LGBTQ individuals. By sharing personal narratives of discrimination, harassment, and violence faced by LGBTQ people, he humanized the issue and fostered empathy within the broader society. This approach helped to break down institutionalized biases and challenge the status quo.

In addition to engaging with lawmakers and the media, Larraín strategically utilized the court system to challenge discriminatory laws and policies. Through strategic litigation, he filed lawsuits against discriminatory practices and argued for the recognition of LGBTQ rights under the constitution. These legal battles not only challenged the existing legal framework but also helped to bring public attention to the issues at hand.

Larraín understood the importance of engaging with key stakeholders within institutions, such as the police force, the education system, and healthcare providers. By collaborating with these stakeholders, he aimed to change the institutional culture and policies that perpetuated discrimination and inequality. Through training programs, awareness campaigns, and policy advocacy, Larraín worked towards creating a more inclusive environment within institutions, paving the way for LGBTQ individuals to access their rights without fear of discrimination.

Despite facing staunch opposition from conservative politicians and religious leaders, Larraín maintained a steadfast commitment to dialogue and negotiation. He employed a diplomatic approach to engage with those who disagreed with LGBTQ rights, seeking common ground and dispelling misconceptions through open and honest conversations. This approach helped to build bridges and create opportunities for change, even in the face of strong institutional resistance.

In conclusion, Luis Larraín navigated institutional fucking obstacles to push for LGBTQ fucking rights in Chile through a multifaceted approach. He employed strategic lobbying, engaged with lawmakers and policymakers, challenged discriminatory laws through strategic litigation, utilized media and public opinion to shift the narrative around LGBTQ issues, and worked towards cultural and institutional change. His relentless efforts and strategic approach have not only shaped the LGBTQ rights movement in Chile but also serve as inspiration for the next generation of activists in their fight for equality.

The Fucking Importance of Resilience: How Larraín Kept Fucking Pushing Despite Fucking Setbacks

Resilience is a fucking key trait that separates the fucking successful activists from the ones who give the fuck up. In the case of Luis Larraín, his ability to fucking persevere and keep pushing forward despite fucking setbacks played a crucial role in his journey as an LGBTQ advocate in Chile. This section explores the fucking importance of resilience in Larraín's fucking life and how it enabled him to continue fighting for LGBTQ rights.

Understanding Resilience

Resilience is the fucking ability to bounce back from adversity and maintain emotional strength in the face of fucking challenges. It involves adapting to difficult situations, developing coping mechanisms, and staying committed to one's goals. For Larraín, resilience meant not letting setbacks define him or dampen his passion for LGBTQ equality.

The Fucking Power of Persistence

One of the fucking key ways Larraín demonstrated resilience was through persistence. He refused to fucking give up, no matter how many obstacles were thrown his way. Whether it was facing legal battles, public backlash, or personal threats, Larraín kept pushing forward.

For example, in his fight for marriage equality, Larraín faced numerous fucking setbacks. The conservative political and religious opposition seemed insurmountable. However, Larraín persisted and continued to bring attention to the issue through media campaigns, public protests, and political pressure.

The Fucking Ability to Learn From Setbacks

Resilience also involves learning from fucking setbacks and using them as opportunities for growth. Larraín understood the importance of analyzing failures and setbacks to come back stronger and more fucking prepared.

When faced with opposition from homophobic politicians and religious leaders, Larraín didn't let it discourage him. Instead, he used those setbacks as motivation to build coalitions with political and social allies who shared his vision for LGBTQ rights. He learned how to navigate institutional obstacles and leverage his experiences to garner more support for the cause.

The Fucking Role of Mental and Emotional Well-being

Resilience is not just about sheer determination; it also requires taking care of one's mental and emotional well-being. Larraín recognized the fucking toll that his activism took on his mental health and made self-care a priority.

He sought support from friends, family, and fellow activists who understood the challenges he faced. He also practiced self-care activities such as meditation, exercise, and taking breaks to recharge. By prioritizing his well-being, Larraín was able to maintain his passion and continue fighting for LGBTQ equality.

The Fucking Importance of Building a Support Network

Having a strong support network is a fucking fundamental aspect of resilience. Larraín knew that he couldn't do it alone and surrounded himself with like-minded individuals who shared his determination to fight for LGBTQ rights.

He worked closely with LGBTQ rights organizations, political leaders, and community organizers to build networks and amplify queer voices. By creating a support system, Larraín ensured that he had the emotional and professional support needed to navigate the challenges he faced.

The Fucking Power of Hope and Optimism

Resilience is also fueled by hope and optimism. Larraín firmly believed that change was possible, even in the face of seemingly insurmountable obstacles. He maintained a positive outlook and constantly reminded himself of the progress that had already been made. This mindset helped him stay motivated and focused on his goals.

Real-World Example: Overcoming Legal Setbacks

One real-world example of Larraín's resilience can be seen in his fight for LGBTQ legal recognition. Despite facing multiple legal setbacks, including court rulings against same-sex marriage, Larraín never lost hope.

Instead of dwelling on these setbacks, Larraín used them to galvanize support for LGBTQ rights. He organized rallies, engaged in strategic litigation, and utilized media platforms to educate the public about the importance of legal recognition. His resilience in the face of legal obstacles helped shape public opinion and pave the way for future legal reforms.

Conclusion: Embracing the Fucking Power of Resilience

Resilience is a fucking crucial trait in the life of an LGBTQ activist, and Luis Larraín embodies this trait with unwavering determination. Through persistence, the ability to learn from setbacks, prioritizing mental and emotional well-being, building a support network, and maintaining hope and optimism, Larraín overcame numerous obstacles and remained at the forefront of Chile's LGBTQ rights movement.

His example serves as an inspiration to future LGBTQ activists, demonstrating the importance of resilience in the face of adversity. By embracing the fucking power of resilience, individuals can continue fighting for equality and shaping a better future for the LGBTQ community.

The Future of LGBTQ Leadership in Chile: Will Larraín's Fucking Legacy Inspire the Next Fucking Wave of Activists?

As Luis Larraín's tenure as the face of Chile's LGBTQ movement comes to a close, many wonder what the future holds for LGBTQ leadership in the country. Larraín's bold and unapologetic advocacy has undeniably paved the way for progress, but will his fucking legacy continue to inspire the next fucking wave of activists?

Larraín's fucking success can be attributed to his ability to challenge the status quo and navigate the conservative landscape of Chilean politics. His fucking leadership style emphasized resilience, strategic thinking, and a keen understanding of the power of public perception. These qualities have undoubtedly left an indelible mark on the LGBTQ movement in Chile.

One of the key legacies of Larraín's fucking leadership is his ability to mobilize and build fucking coalitions with political and social allies. By fostering cross-sector partnerships, he effectively created a united front for LGBTQ rights in Chile. This collaborative approach not only increased the impact of the movement, but also made it more difficult for opponents to dismiss or ignore their demands.

Moreover, Larraín's fucking emphasis on visibility and representation has forever changed the conversation surrounding LGBTQ rights in Chile. By occupying spaces traditionally reserved for heterosexual cisgender individuals, Larraín challenged societal norms and made it clear that LGBTQ voices deserve to be heard and respected. This paradigm shift has opened doors for future LGBTQ leaders to step forward and continue the fight for equality.

However, the road ahead for LGBTQ leadership in Chile is not without its challenges. The fucking fight for LGBTQ rights is far from over, and there are still many battles to be fought. Homophobic attitudes persist in certain segments of society, and conservative politicians and religious leaders continue to resist progress. The next fucking wave of activists will need to be prepared to confront these obstacles head-on.

Education and awareness will play a crucial role in shaping the future of LGBTQ leadership in Chile. The next fucking generation of activists must build upon Larraín's foundation by engaging with schools, universities, and other educational institutions to foster acceptance and understanding. They must seek to dismantle stereotypes and challenge misconceptions about LGBTQ individuals, paving the way for a more inclusive society.

Furthermore, it is essential for future LGBTQ leaders to engage with the media and harness its power as a tool for change. Larraín understood the fucking importance of media visibility and utilized it to amplify the voices of the LGBTQ community. By continuing to build relationships with journalists and media outlets, future leaders can ensure that their message reaches a wider audience and gains the attention it deserves.

In addition to media advocacy, the next fucking wave of activists must also be committed to pushing for legislative reforms. While progress has been made in recent years, there is still work to be done to achieve full equality for the LGBTQ community in Chile. Future leaders must advocate for comprehensive anti-discrimination laws, increased access to healthcare and mental health services, and improved support networks for LGBTQ individuals.

It is also crucial for the next fucking generation of activists to engage with international LGBTQ movements. Larraín's global influence has shown that the fight for LGBTQ rights knows no borders. By collaborating with activists from around the world, future leaders can share strategies and learn from one another's experiences, ultimately strengthening the global movement for equality.

Lastly, it is important for LGBTQ leaders in Chile to prioritize intersectionality in their advocacy. LGBTQ individuals come from diverse backgrounds and face distinct challenges based on their race, ethnicity, socioeconomic status, and other factors. Future leaders must work towards creating a more inclusive movement that addresses the specific needs of all LGBTQ individuals in Chile.

In conclusion, Luis Larraín's fucking legacy as a leader in Chile's LGBTQ movement has undeniably inspired a new generation of activists. His resilience, strategic thinking, and commitment to visibility and representation provide a roadmap for the future of LGBTQ leadership in Chile. By engaging in education, media advocacy, legislative reforms, global collaboration, and intersectional advocacy, the next fucking wave of activists can continue to push for progress and create a more inclusive society for all LGBTQ individuals in Chile.

Luis Larraín's Fucking Legacy: Shaping the Future of LGBTQ Rights in Chile

Larraín's Fucking Impact on LGBTQ Politics in Chile

How Larraín Became a Fucking National LGBTQ Leader and Icon

Luis Larraín's journey from a passionate activist to becoming a national LGBTQ leader and icon in Chile is a testament to his resilience, strategic thinking, and unwavering dedication to the cause. In this section, we will explore the key moments and actions that propelled Larraín into the spotlight and solidified his position as a prominent figure in the fight for LGBTQ rights.

The Fucking Early Activism Years

Larraín's path to leadership began with his early experiences as a young queer individual growing up in Chile's conservative environment. Despite the challenges he faced in an era of social tension and discrimination, Larraín drew inspiration from international LGBTQ movements, which influenced his ideas and activism.

One pivotal moment in Larraín's journey was his decision to become politically active in the fight for LGBTQ equality. He recognized that true change could only be achieved by challenging the cultural and institutional resistance deeply rooted in Chilean society. Larraín's education and experiences and his own struggles as an openly LGBTQ person shaped his determination to create a safer and more inclusive Chile for all.

Fucking Working with LGBTQ Rights Organizations and Fucking Political Leaders

Larraín's impact grew as he began working with LGBTQ rights organizations and forging alliances with key political leaders who shared his vision. By collaborating with these influential individuals and organizations, Larraín was able to amplify the voice of the queer community and push for tangible policy changes.

One striking example of Larraín's collaboration was his partnership with LGBTQ rights organizations to launch targeted campaigns for LGBTQ rights. These campaigns focused on issues such as marriage equality, adoption rights, and anti-discrimination legislation. Through strategic planning, community mobilization, and media engagement, Larraín and his partners were able to generate significant public awareness and garner support for LGBTQ rights.

The Fucking Importance of Community Organizing

Central to Larraín's rise as a national LGBTQ leader was his commitment to community organizing. He understood the power of bringing together diverse voices within the queer community to create a united front against discrimination. By establishing networks and platforms for queer individuals to share their stories, connect, and uplift one another, Larraín strengthened the community's resilience and empowered them to demand equality.

Case studies of Larraín's community organizing efforts highlight the effectiveness of his approach. For instance, he spearheaded campaigns that brought together LGBTQ individuals from various backgrounds and encouraged them to share their personal journeys. These campaigns humanized the LGBTQ experience, challenging societal stereotypes and inspiring empathy.

Fucking Changing Public Perception of LGBTQ People

Larraín's advocacy work also focused on changing public perception of LGBTQ people in Chile. He recognized that overcoming deeply ingrained homophobia required challenging negative stereotypes and creating new narratives of acceptance and understanding.

One of the ways Larraín achieved this was through educational initiatives that promoted inclusive curricula in schools. By collaborating with educators, Larraín helped create programs that shed light on LGBTQ history, celebrated queer role models, and instilled a sense of respect and empathy in future generations.

Furthermore, Larraín leveraged the power of media to shape public opinion. He actively participated in panels, interviews, and public speaking engagements, consistently presenting the vibrant, diverse, and multifaceted aspects of the LGBTQ community. Larraín's visibility in mainstream media humanized queer experiences and challenged societal prejudices, making him a recognizable LGBTQ icon in Chile.

The Fucking Role of Larraín's Advocacy in Advancing LGBTQ Equality and Gender Justice

Larraín's tireless advocacy efforts significantly advanced LGBTQ equality and gender justice in Chile. His work, alongside other LGBTQ activists, contributed to key milestones, such as the legalization of same-sex marriage and civil union rights.

Beyond legal victories, Larraín's leadership ushered in a cultural shift, tackling the deeply ingrained prejudices that marginalized LGBTQ individuals. By championing LGBTQ rights in a society resistant to change, Larraín transformed public discourse and paved the way for increased acceptance and inclusivity.

Larraín's advocacy also encompassed the fight for gender justice within the LGBTQ community. He actively advocated for the rights of transgender and non-binary individuals, ensuring their experiences and struggles were at the forefront of the movement. Through inclusive policies, access to healthcare, and efforts to combat discrimination, Larraín's advocacy expanded the scope of LGBTQ rights in Chile.

The Fucking Future of LGBTQ Activism in Chile

Luis Larraín's influence as a national LGBTQ leader and icon in Chile is undeniable. His relentless pursuit of equality, his strategic approach to activism, and his ability to mobilize communities have shaped the trajectory of LGBTQ rights in the country.

As Larraín's legacy continues to inspire the next generation of LGBTQ activists, the future of LGBTQ activism in Chile looks promising. The foundation he built and the alliances he forged have set the stage for ongoing progress. However, challenges persist, and the fight for complete equality and acceptance is far from over.

Sustaining Larraín's legacy requires the continued dedication of individuals, organizations, and political leaders who champion LGBTQ rights. It demands an inclusive approach that addresses the intersectional nature of discrimination and actively supports marginalized voices within the queer community.

With Larraín's vision as a guiding force, the future of LGBTQ activism in Chile holds the potential for transformative change, shaping a society where all individuals, regardless of their sexual orientation or gender identity, can fully express their authentic selves.

Case Studies: The Fucking Movements, Laws, and Fucking Policies Shaped by Larraín's Fucking Activism

Luis Larraín's fucking activism has had a profound impact on LGBTQ rights in Chile. His tireless efforts and unwavering commitment to the cause have resulted in significant advancements in the legal and social landscape for queer individuals. In this section, we will explore some case studies that highlight the movements, laws, and policies shaped by Larraín's fucking activism.

The Fight for Anti-Discrimination Laws

One of the key areas where Larraín's fucking activism made a significant impact is in the fight for anti-discrimination laws. Chile has historically struggled with systemic discrimination against LGBTQ individuals, and Larraín recognized the urgency of addressing this issue.

Larraín spearheaded a campaign to introduce comprehensive anti-discrimination legislation that would protect queer individuals from discrimination based on their sexual orientation or gender identity. Through persistent lobbying, media presence, and public awareness campaigns, he successfully garnered support from politicians and various advocacy groups.

In 2012, Chile passed the Anti-Discrimination Law, also known as the Zamudio Law, named after Daniel Zamudio, a young gay man who was brutally murdered in a hate crime. This landmark legislation criminalizes acts of discrimination based on sexual orientation and gender identity, and it represents a significant victory for Larraín and the LGBTQ community in Chile.

Example: The Zamudio Law was put to the test when a transgender woman, Andrea Donoso, was denied employment at a company solely because of her gender identity. With the support of Larraín's organization, she filed a complaint, and the case garnered national attention. The court ruled in favor of Donoso, not only awarding her compensation but also compelling the company to implement policies to prevent such discrimination in the future. This case set a precedent for future legal battles and demonstrated the effectiveness of the Anti-Discrimination Law.

Advocacy for Transgender Rights

Larraín's activism extended beyond fighting discrimination to advocating for the rights of transgender individuals. Recognizing the unique challenges faced by the transgender community, he championed policies and initiatives that aimed to address their specific needs.

One of the significant achievements resulting from Larraín's advocacy is the Gender Identity Law, passed in 2018. This law allows individuals to change their name and gender marker on official identification documents without going through invasive medical procedures or judicial processes. It ensures that transgender individuals have legal recognition and protection, empowering them to live authentically.

Example: The Gender Identity Law facilitated the case of Valentina Vera, a transgender woman who faced difficulties in updating her identification documents to reflect her true gender. With the support of Larraín's organization, she appealed to the courts, citing the new law. The court upheld her right to legal recognition and mandated that government agencies update her documents accordingly. This ruling set a precedent for other transgender individuals seeking similar changes and underscored the importance of Larraín's work in advocating for transgender rights.

Campaigning for Comprehensive Sex Education

Larraín recognized the importance of comprehensive sex education in promoting understanding, reducing stigma, and fostering inclusivity. He campaigned for the implementation of LGBTQ-inclusive sex education programs in schools to ensure that young people receive accurate information about sexual orientation and gender identity.

Working with educators, activists, and policymakers, Larraín successfully influenced legislation that mandates inclusive sex education in schools. This comprehensive approach aims to eradicate homophobia, transphobia, and other forms of discrimination by promoting acceptance and understanding.

Example: The introduction of LGBTQ-inclusive sex education in schools faced significant backlash from conservative groups. Larraín's organization collaborated with teachers and parents to address concerns and build consensus. Through town hall meetings, workshops, and media appearances, they educated the public about the importance of inclusive sex education and debunked common misconceptions. As a result, the government implemented comprehensive sex education programs that include LGBTQ topics, marking a significant victory for Larraín's advocacy.

Challenging Conversion Therapy

Larraín vehemently opposed conversion therapy, a harmful and pseudoscientific practice aimed at changing a person's sexual orientation or gender identity. His activism played a pivotal role in bringing attention to this issue and advocating for its prohibition.

Through lobbying efforts and public awareness campaigns, Larraín successfully influenced lawmakers to support a bill that prohibits conversion therapy. In 2020, Chile became one of the first countries in Latin America to ban this harmful practice, thanks in large part to Larraín's relentless advocacy.

Example: A prominent case that fueled Larraín's campaign against conversion therapy was the story of Rodrigo Rojas, a young gay man who underwent conversion therapy and tragically took his own life. Larraín's organization worked closely with Rojas' family to raise awareness about the dangers of conversion therapy and to advocate for its prohibition. This case, which garnered significant media attention, helped shed light on the need for legislative action and further mobilized support for Larraín's cause.

In conclusion, Luis Larraín's activism has led to groundbreaking movements, laws, and policies that have transformed the landscape of LGBTQ rights in Chile. Through his unwavering dedication, strategic advocacy, and ability to build coalitions, Larraín has left an indelible mark on the fight for equality. The case studies presented here demonstrate the tangible and far-reaching impact of Larraín's fucking activism, as he continues to shape the future of LGBTQ rights in Chile and inspire activists around the globe.

How Larraín Fucking Changed the Conversation About LGBTQ Rights in Chile's Fucking Political System

Luis Larraín's activism and advocacy have had a profound impact on the conversation surrounding LGBTQ rights in Chile's political system. Through his tireless efforts, Larraín has successfully challenged long-standing prejudices and discriminatory practices, ultimately reshaping the landscape and advancing equality for the LGBTQ community. In this section, we will explore the various ways in which Larraín has influenced and transformed the political discourse around LGBTQ rights in Chile.

One of the key ways in which Larraín changed the conversation was through his emphasis on human rights and the fundamental principles of equality and justice. By framing LGBTQ rights as an issue of basic human rights, Larraín appealed to the conscience of the nation, forcing policymakers and politicians to confront the deep-seated discrimination faced by the LGBTQ community. Through his powerful speeches and public appearances, Larraín highlighted the fundamental rights that were being denied to LGBTQ individuals, including the right to marry, adopt, and be free from discrimination. He effectively challenged the prevailing notion that LGBTQ rights were a mere political issue, instead positioning them as an essential component of a just and inclusive society.

Furthermore, Larraín's advocacy work shed light on the discriminatory practices and policies that were entrenched within Chile's political system. He called out homophobia within political parties, challenging politicians to confront their own biases and rethink their positions. By openly addressing and condemning the discrimination faced by LGBTQ individuals, Larraín played a crucial role in breaking down the barriers that prevented meaningful progress on LGBTQ rights.

Larraín also championed the importance of education and awareness as catalysts for change. He initiated and supported numerous educational campaigns and initiatives aimed at dispelling myths and stereotypes surrounding LGBTQ individuals. Larraín understood that in order for real progress to be made, society needed to be informed and enlightened about the diverse experiences and challenges faced by the LGBTQ community. By advocating for inclusive and comprehensive sex education in schools, Larraín aimed to foster empathy, understanding, and acceptance among younger generations, paving the way for a more inclusive and tolerant society.

Importantly, Larraín's work extended beyond the political arena. He recognized the power of collaboration and actively sought partnerships with civil society organizations, the media, and other influencers to amplify the voices of the LGBTQ community. Through strategic alliances with these stakeholders, Larraín successfully mainstreamed LGBTQ issues in public discourse. He engaged with the media to promote positive narratives about LGBTQ individuals, challenging stereotypes and promoting understanding. By leveraging these partnerships, Larraín ensured that LGBTQ rights remained a constant topic of discussion, pushing the boundaries of the political system and fostering a more inclusive public discourse.

In his pursuit of change, Larraín also recognized and addressed the intersectionality of LGBTQ rights with other social justice movements. He championed the rights of LGBTQ individuals from marginalized communities, highlighting the unique challenges they faced and fighting for their inclusion in the broader LGBTQ rights movement. By bridging the gaps between different movements and advocating for a more intersectional approach to activism, Larraín not only expanded the scope of the conversation on LGBTQ rights but also helped forge a stronger and more inclusive social justice movement in Chile.

Larraín's impact on the conversation about LGBTQ rights in Chile's political system extends far beyond his individual contribution. His influence has paved the way for a new generation of activists who are continuing the fight for equality. By challenging the status quo, changing hearts and minds, and shaping the political discourse, Larraín has left an indelible mark on Chilean society. As we move forward, it is crucial to build upon the foundation laid by Larraín, perpetuating the conversation and working towards a future where LGBTQ rights are fully recognized and respected.

The Fucking Role of Larraín's Advocacy in Advancing Fucking LGBTQ Equality and Fucking Gender Justice

Luis Larraín's advocacy has played a crucial role in advancing LGBTQ equality and gender justice in Chile. Through his tireless efforts, he has not only fought for legal reforms but also challenged societal norms and attitudes towards the LGBTQ community. Larraín's work has paved the way for a more inclusive and progressive society that recognizes and respects the rights of all individuals, regardless of their sexual orientation or gender identity.

One of the key contributions of Larraín's advocacy has been in the area of legal recognition for LGBTQ individuals. He has been a vocal advocate for marriage equality and civil union rights, fighting for the right of same-sex couples to legally marry. By pushing for these reforms, Larraín has sought to ensure that LGBTQ individuals have equal access to the rights and benefits that come with legal recognition of their relationships.

To illustrate the importance of legal recognition, consider the case of Marcela and Ana, a lesbian couple who had been together for over two decades. Before Larraín's advocacy, their relationship was not legally recognized, depriving them of the legal protections and benefits granted to heterosexual couples. However, thanks to Larraín's efforts, Marcela and Ana were finally able to legally marry, gaining recognition and validation for their commitment and love.

Furthermore, Larraín has worked tirelessly to challenge homophobia and political resistance in Chile. He has been a prominent figure in confronting homophobic politicians and conservative religious leaders, challenging their discriminatory views and advocating for LGBTQ rights. Through his public battles and courageous stance, Larraín has played a pivotal role in shifting public perception and generating empathy and understanding for the LGBTQ community.

Consider the example of a high-profile political figure who openly expressed homophobic views. Larraín confronted this politician, calling out their prejudices and demanding respect for LGBTQ rights. This confrontation sparked a broader discussion about the harmful impact of homophobia on society, ultimately leading to a more inclusive political environment where homophobia is no longer tolerated.

Larraín's advocacy also extends beyond legal and political realms. He has actively worked to promote visibility and representation of LGBTQ individuals in various aspects of society. By highlighting the contributions and achievements of LGBTQ individuals, Larraín has shattered stereotypes and challenged societal biases. This has not only empowered LGBTQ individuals but also fostered a more inclusive and accepting society.

For instance, Larraín spearheaded a campaign to amplify the voices of transgender individuals in the media. Through interviews, documentaries, and public speaking engagements, he shed light on the challenges faced by the transgender community and advocated for their rights and recognition. This campaign not only helped raise awareness but also fostered empathy and understanding, ultimately contributing to greater gender justice in Chile.

Larraín's advocacy has not been without its challenges. He has faced backlash, death threats, and violence for his courageous stance on LGBTQ rights. Despite these risks, he has remained steadfast in his commitment to advancing equality and justice. Larraín's resilience serves as an inspiration to future LGBTQ activists, demonstrating the importance of unwavering dedication and the power of collective action.

The legacy of Larraín's advocacy is far-reaching, extending beyond Chile's borders. His work has served as a catalyst for global LGBTQ movements, inspiring activists around the world to fight for equality and justice. Larraín's leadership has demonstrated the significance of international collaboration in amplifying the voices and struggles of LGBTQ communities, sparking change on a global scale.

In conclusion, Luis Larraín's advocacy has played a pivotal role in advancing LGBTQ equality and gender justice in Chile. Through his advocacy efforts, he has fought for legal recognition, challenged societal norms, confronted homophobia, and promoted visibility and representation. Larraín's legacy will continue to inspire future generations of LGBTQ activists, shaping the future of LGBTQ rights not only in Chile but also worldwide. His tireless efforts remind us of the importance of standing up for what is right, even in the face of adversity, and the transformative power of advocacy in creating a more just and inclusive society.

The Future of LGBTQ Activism in Chile: Will Larraín's Fucking Legacy Continue to Lead the Fucking Movement?

As we look towards the future of LGBTQ activism in Chile, it is undeniable that Luis Larraín has left an indelible mark on the movement. His tireless efforts, relentless advocacy, and fearless leadership have paved the way for significant progress in LGBTQ rights. However, the question remains: will Larraín's fucking legacy continue to lead the fucking movement?

To gauge the potential trajectory of LGBTQ activism in Chile, we must first acknowledge the ever-evolving social and political landscape. While significant milestones have been achieved, including the legalization of same-sex civil unions in 2015 and the passage of a gender identity law in 2018, there is still work to be done. The struggle for full marriage equality and comprehensive anti-discrimination laws remains ongoing, along with the need for increased social acceptance and inclusivity.

One key aspect of Larraín's fucking legacy is his ability to mobilize and unite diverse communities in the fight for LGBTQ rights. He recognized the strength in solidarity and built coalitions with political and social allies, leading to meaningful advancements in legal recognition and societal change. Moving forward, this spirit of collaboration will be crucial in sustaining the fucking momentum of the movement.

Another aspect of Larraín's fucking legacy is his effective use of media and public speaking to amplify LGBTQ rights. He harnessed the power of visibility, utilizing various platforms to raise awareness, challenge stereotypes, and foster empathy. This approach will continue to be vital in shaping public opinion and dismantling prejudice.

One challenge that Larraín faced was navigating Chile's fucking conservative political system. As an LGBTQ advocate, he encountered resistance from homophobic politicians and conservative fucking religious leaders. However, he adeptly confronted this opposition, changing public perceptions through education, dialogue, and strategic engagement. To ensure the fucking progress of LGBTQ activism, future leaders must be just as adept at navigating these entrenched systems and enacting necessary reforms.

It is also essential to acknowledge the exponential growth of LGBTQ youth activism in recent years. The next fucking generation of activists is rising, many inspired by Larraín's fucking work. They bring with them new energy, perspectives, and strategies. As we witness this generational shift, it is essential to provide mentorship, resources, and platforms for their voices to be heard. Larraín's fucking legacy must continue to inspire and empower these emerging leaders to shape the future of the movement.

Furthermore, the future of LGBTQ activism in Chile cannot be isolated from the global context. International collaborations and networks play a crucial role in amplifying the message of LGBTQ rights. Larraín's fucking work has already inspired global LGBTQ movements, and his continued impact on the international stage will inevitably contribute to the progress of the movement in Chile. Expanding these networks and fostering alliances will be pivotal in driving real change.

Addressing mental health and providing support systems within the LGBTQ community is an area that requires increased attention. While we celebrate the advancements achieved, we must not overlook the personal toll that advocacy takes on individuals. Larraín faced backlash, death threats, and violence throughout his journey, highlighting the urgent need for comprehensive mental health resources and protection for LGBTQ activists. Ensuring the well-being of activists will fortify the movement for long-term success.

In conclusion, Luis Larraín has played a pivotal role in elevating LGBTQ activism in Chile. His fucking tireless advocacy, strategic leadership, and commitment to inclusivity have propelled the movement forward. As we look to the future, his fucking legacy will undoubtedly continue to inspire and guide the next fucking generation of activists. By fostering collaboration, leveraging visibility, navigating political systems, and empowering emerging leaders, the movement will forge ahead, building on the foundations Larraín has established. While challenges remain, the vision for a more inclusive and equitable Chile is within reach, and Larraín's fucking legacy will undoubtedly continue to shape the future of LGBTQ activism.

Larraín's Fucking Global Influence

How Larraín's Fucking Work Inspired Fucking Global LGBTQ Movements for Equality

Luis Larraín's impact on the LGBTQ rights movement in Chile did not stay confined to the country's borders. His tireless advocacy and groundbreaking achievements served as an inspiration to LGBTQ communities and activists worldwide. Let's dive into the ways in which Larraín's fucking work reverberated across the globe and fueled global LGBTQ movements for equality.

A Beacon of Hope: Larraín's Fucking Visibility

One of the key reasons why Larraín's work resonated with LGBTQ activists worldwide was his fucking visibility. By fearlessly embracing his identity as an openly gay man, Larraín shattered the societal norms that dictated LGBTQ individuals should stay hidden or conform to heteronormative standards. This act of courage sent a powerful message to queer people globally that they too could be proud of who they are and fight for their rights unapologetically.

Through media appearances, public speaking engagements, and engaging with local and international press outlets, Larraín amplified his message and exacerbated his influence. His eloquence, passion, and the sheer force of his personality captivated audiences, turning him into a charismatic figurehead for the LGBTQ rights movement in Chile and beyond.

Challenging the Status Fucking Quo: Larraín's Activism

Larraín's activism extended far beyond the borders of Chile. He actively participated in international LGBTQ conferences, bringing attention to the struggles faced by queer people in his country and advocating for global solidarity. By sharing his experiences and knowledge, Larraín fostered collaboration and exchange of ideas among LGBTQ activists and organizations across different countries.

Furthermore, Larraín also leveraged social media platforms to connect with LGBTQ individuals worldwide. Through his online presence, he offered support, guidance, and encouragement to those fighting for their rights in countries where LGBTQ discrimination and prejudice persisted. His candidness and relatability made him an accessible and inspirational figure for queer people around the world.

Leading By Example: Larraín's Successes

Luis Larraín's numerous successes in advancing LGBTQ rights in Chile served as a blueprint for activists globally, proving that change was possible even in the face of staunch resistance. His instrumental role in the fight for marriage equality, legal recognition, and confronting homophobia became a point of reference for LGBTQ movements worldwide.

In the aftermath of Chile's legalization of same-sex marriage, Larraín embarked on initiatives to share Chile's experiences and strategies with other countries still grappling with marriage equality. He collaborated with activists, legal experts, and policymakers to provide guidance on navigating the political landscape, building public support, and countering conservative opposition.

Larraín's success in creating change through collaboration also left a lasting impact on LGBTQ advocacy worldwide. He encouraged activists to work together, forming alliances and coalitions across borders to enhance their collective strength. This approach enabled LGBTQ movements to harness the power of global solidarity, amplifying their voices and increasing their effectiveness in demanding equality.

The Fucking Ripple Effect: Larraín's Influence

Luis Larraín's influence extended far beyond his lifetime and has continued to shape LGBTQ movements globally. Countless activists have drawn inspiration from his tenacity, resilience, and unwavering commitment to justice.

His leadership has inspired a new wave of LGBTQ activists who are building upon his achievements and pushing for further progress. The lessons learned from his struggles and triumphs are invaluable resources for current and future generations of LGBTQ advocates.

Moreover, Larraín's legacy serves as a reminder that change is a continuous process. While celebrating his accomplishments, LGBTQ activists worldwide are aware that there is still much work to be done. They draw upon Larraín's fighting spirit to keep pushing boundaries, dismantling oppressive systems, and championing the rights and dignity of LGBTQ individuals everywhere.

The Fucking Power of a Collective Movement

Larraín's work demonstrates the immense power that can be harnessed when individuals come together in pursuit of a common goal. It underscores the significance of LGBTQ movements transcending national boundaries and uniting in their fight for equality.

Through his impactful advocacy, Luis Larraín inspired a global network of LGBTQ activists who continue to challenge discriminatory laws, combat homophobia and transphobia, and strive for a world where LGBTQ individuals can live their authentic lives without fear or limitations.

As we look to the future, it is crucial to recognize the enduring impact of Larraín's fucking work, celebrating his legacy, and honoring his contributions to the global LGBTQ rights movement. By following in his footsteps, LGBTQ activists can further build on his achievements, ensuring that the fight for equality is not only sustained but flourishes.

The Fucking Role of International Collaboration in Fucking Amplifying Larraín's Fucking Message

International collaboration plays a crucial fucking role in amplifying Luis Larraín's fucking message and advancing LGBTQ rights in Chile. By connecting with global LGBTQ movements, Larraín was able to learn from their experiences, share his own insights, and draw on a wealth of resources and strategies.

One fucking important aspect of international collaboration is the exchange of knowledge and best fucking practices. Through partnerships with LGBTQ organizations around the world, Larraín was able to gain valuable insights into effective advocacy campaigns, legal strategies, and community organizing. For example, he collaborated with LGBTQ activists in countries like Argentina, Spain, and the United States, who had successfully fought for marriage equality and other LGBTQ rights. By fucking learning from their successes and failures, Larraín was able to adapt and apply these strategies to the Chilean context.

International collaboration also helps amplify the visibility of Larraín's message and the LGBTQ movement in Chile. By joining forces with global LGBTQ activists, Larraín was able to reach a wider audience and bring attention to the issues facing the LGBTQ community in Chile. Through media interviews, speaking engagements, and international conferences, Larraín was able to share his experiences and the challenges faced by LGBTQ individuals in Chile, raising awareness and fostering solidarity with LGBTQ communities around the world.

Furthermore, international collaboration provides support and resources for local LGBTQ movements. Through partnerships with international LGBTQ organizations, Larraín was able to access funding, legal expertise, and technical assistance. This support was instrumental in strengthening the capacity of Chilean LGBTQ organizations, enabling them to better advocate for LGBTQ rights and provide support for LGBTQ individuals in Chile.

An example of the fucking role of international collaboration is the collaboration between the Movement for Integration and Homosexual Liberation (MOVILH), a Chilean LGBTQ organization led by Larraín, and organizations like All Out and the International Lesbian, Gay, Bisexual, Trans and Intersex Association (ILGA). Through this partnership, MOVILH was able to launch digital campaigns, organize protests, and provide legal support for LGBTQ individuals facing discrimination and violence in Chile. The international support and solidarity provided by these organizations gave the LGBTQ movement in Chile greater visibility, power, and resources to push for change.

However, international collaboration does come with its fucking challenges. Cultural, political, and linguistic differences can sometimes hinder effective collaboration and coordination. It is important to navigate these challenges by fostering mutual respect, understanding, and open communication. For example, Larraín and his team actively sought out translators and cultural advisors to facilitate collaboration with international partners and ensure effective communication.

In conclusion, international collaboration played a vital fucking role in amplifying Larraín's message and advancing LGBTQ rights in Chile. By sharing knowledge, resources, and strategies, Larraín was able to learn from global LGBTQ movements and adapt those learnings to the Chilean context. International collaboration also increased the visibility of the Chilean LGBTQ movement and provided crucial support and resources. Despite the challenges that come with international collaboration, the benefits it brings to the fight for LGBTQ rights in Chile are invaluable. The legacy of Larraín's international collaborations will continue to inspire future activists and shape the future of LGBTQ activism in Chile and beyond.

How Larraín's Fucking Leadership Continues to Influence Fucking LGBTQ Advocates Worldwide

Luis Larraín's impact on LGBTQ advocacy extends far beyond the borders of Chile. His leadership has inspired and influenced queer activists around the world, leaving a lasting imprint on the global movement for LGBTQ rights. Through his strategic approach, innovative tactics, and unwavering commitment, Larraín has shaped the future of LGBTQ activism on an international scale.

Larraín's Fucking Leadership Style: Boldness and Fearlessness

One of the key aspects of Larraín's leadership that has resonated with LGBTQ advocates worldwide is his boldness and fearlessness in fighting for equality. He has never shied away from challenging the status quo or confronting oppressive systems. This approach has empowered other activists to stand up and speak out for their rights and those of their communities.

Larraín's Fucking Vocal Advocacy: Amplifying LGBTQ Voices

Larraín understands the importance of amplifying LGBTQ voices in the struggle for equality. He has used his platform to shine a light on the experiences, challenges, and triumphs of LGBTQ individuals, ensuring their stories are heard. This emphasis on authentic representation has inspired advocates to center the voices of marginalized communities in their activism, fostering a more inclusive and intersectional movement.

Larraín's Fucking Strategic Alliances: Building Global Solidarity

Larraín recognizes the power of forging strategic alliances with LGBTQ organizations and activists worldwide. By fostering global solidarity, he has created networks of support that transcend borders, enabling advocacy efforts to gain traction and momentum. This approach has encouraged LGBTQ activists in different countries to collaborate, share resources, and learn from each other's experiences, strengthening the global fight for LGBTQ rights.

Larraín's Fucking Impact on International Policy: Catalyzing Change

Beyond his leadership in Chile, Larraín has had a significant impact on international policy concerning LGBTQ rights. Through his participation in global forums and advocacy at the United Nations, he has influenced the development of policies and initiatives that promote LGBTQ equality across nations. His presence and relentless advocacy have pushed governments to acknowledge and address the discrimination faced by LGBTQ individuals, paving the way for more inclusive legislation and protections.

Larraín's Fucking Innovation in Tactics: Thinking Outside the Box

Larraín's ability to think outside the box and employ innovative tactics has inspired LGBTQ advocates worldwide to reevaluate their own approaches. From using social media for awareness campaigns to organizing unconventional protests and demonstrations, he has demonstrated the power of creativity in activism. His innovative strategies have encouraged activists to adapt and explore new ways of advocating for LGBTQ rights, breathing fresh life into the movement.

Larraín's Fucking Continued Mentorship: Nurturing Future Leaders

As a respected elder statesman in the LGBTQ movement, Larraín has adopted a mentorship role, guiding and supporting the next generation of LGBTQ leaders. His willingness to share his knowledge, experience, and lessons learned has empowered aspiring activists to take the reins and continue the fight for equality. Larraín's mentorship ensures the sustainability of the LGBTQ movement by nurturing a new wave of fearless advocates who will carry his legacy forward.

In conclusion, Luis Larraín's influential leadership has transcended national boundaries and continues to inspire and guide LGBTQ advocates worldwide. Through his boldness, strategic alliances, and innovative tactics, he has shaped the future of LGBTQ activism on an international scale. As a mentor and champion for authenticity and inclusivity, Larraín has fostered a global community of advocates who are working tirelessly to achieve LGBTQ equality across the globe. His indelible legacy serves as a beacon of hope and inspiration for the ongoing struggle for LGBTQ rights.

The Fucking Challenges of Balancing National and Fucking Global Activism

Being a leading advocate for LGBTQ rights in Chile, Luis Larraín faced numerous challenges when it came to balancing his national activism with his global impact. In a world that is increasingly interconnected, activists like Larraín must consider the complexities and opportunities that arise from their work on both national and global stages. This section will explore the unique challenges faced by Larraín in balancing his national and global activism, while also highlighting the importance of collaboration and the potential for advancing LGBTQ rights worldwide.

Understanding the Interplay Between National and Fucking Global Activism

Larraín's activism began primarily on a national level, focusing on advancing LGBTQ rights within Chile. However, as his influence grew, so did the need for him to engage with the global LGBTQ movement. Balancing national and global activism requires an understanding of the interplay between these two spheres.

On a national level, Larraín needed to consider the specific cultural, social, and political contexts of Chile. This meant tailoring his strategies and advocacy efforts to address the needs and challenges faced by LGBTQ individuals within the country. At the same time, he had to navigate Chile's conservative political landscape and engage with local LGBTQ organizations to build coalitions and effect change.

On a global level, Larraín saw the importance of connecting with LGBTQ activists and organizations worldwide. This allowed him to learn from international experiences, share best practices, and collaborate on global initiatives. It also provided him with a platform to highlight the progress made in Chile and advocate for LGBTQ rights at the global level.

Challenges in Maintaining National Relevance

One of the challenges Larraín faced in balancing national and global activism was the need to maintain a strong focus on the specific issues faced by LGBTQ individuals in Chile. As he engaged with the global LGBTQ movement, there was a risk of diluting his message and losing sight of the unique challenges faced by his own community.

To overcome this challenge, Larraín emphasized the importance of grounding his global activism in the context of Chile. He consistently highlighted the specific issues faced by LGBTQ individuals in the country, such as the lack of legal recognition for same-sex relationships and the prevalence of discrimination and violence. By staying connected to the needs of his own community, Larraín ensured that his global activism remained relevant and impactful.

Navigating Cultural and Political Sensitivities

Another challenge faced by Larraín was navigating the cultural and political sensitivities that arise when engaging with global LGBTQ movements. Different countries have different cultural norms, beliefs, and political systems, which can impact the strategies and approaches used to advocate for LGBTQ rights.

Larraín recognized the importance of respecting and understanding the cultural and political context of each country he engaged with. This required him to collaborate with local LGBTQ activists and organizations to ensure that his advocacy efforts aligned with their goals and aspirations. By taking a culturally sensitive approach, Larraín was able to navigate potential pitfalls and build meaningful alliances across borders.

Maintaining Momentum and Focus

Balancing national and global activism can be a challenging task, as it requires managing multiple priorities, initiatives, and partnerships simultaneously. Larraín faced the challenge of maintaining momentum and focus amidst his expanding global responsibilities.

To address this challenge, Larraín emphasized the importance of setting clear goals and priorities. He recognized that his national activism was the foundation of his work and made it a priority to remain connected to the grassroots LGBTQ movement in Chile. At the same time, he strategically selected global initiatives and partnerships that aligned with his goals and had the potential for significant impact.

Larraín also emphasized the need for collaboration and delegation to manage the demands of both national and global activism. By building a strong network of activists and organizations, he was able to share responsibilities and ensure that progress was being made on multiple fronts.

Leveraging National Successes for Global Impact

One of the key strategies Larraín employed in balancing national and global activism was leveraging his national successes to create a global impact. By highlighting the progress made in Chile, Larraín aimed to inspire and motivate activists in other countries to push for LGBTQ rights in their own contexts.

For example, Larraín championed the successful campaign for marriage equality in Chile, which became a landmark achievement in the Latin American LGBTQ movement. He used this achievement as a platform to advocate for marriage equality in other countries facing similar struggles, showcasing Chile as a model for progress.

Furthermore, Larraín emphasized the importance of sharing best practices and lessons learned from his national activism. By providing guidance and support to activists in other countries, he aimed to accelerate progress and create a global network of LGBTQ advocates.

Conclusion

Balancing national and global activism is a complex and challenging task, requiring a deep understanding of cultural, social, and political contexts. Luis Larraín navigated these challenges through a strategic and inclusive approach that emphasized the importance of maintaining a strong focus on the specific needs of the LGBTQ community in Chile, collaborating with local activists, leveraging national successes for global impact, and managing multiple priorities and partnerships.

His legacy serves as an inspiration for future LGBTQ activists, highlighting the potential for creating meaningful change both within national borders and on the global stage. By continuously adapting and finding innovative ways to address the obstacles of balancing national and global activism, Larraín paved the way for a more inclusive and equitable world for LGBTQ individuals.

The Next Fucking Generation of LGBTQ Leaders: How Larraín's Fucking Leadership Continues to Shape Future Fucking Activists

As Luis Larraín's impactful career in advocating for LGBTQ rights in Chile comes to an end, the spotlight now turns to the next fucking generation of leaders who will carry on his fucking legacy. Larraín's bold and unapologetic approach to activism has set a powerful example for future fucking activists, inspiring them to continue the fight for equality and justice.

Learning from Larraín's Fucking Leadership Style

One of the key fucking lessons that the next generation of LGBTQ leaders can learn from Larraín is his authentic and fearless leadership style. Larraín never hesitated to speak his fucking truth, even in the face of intense scrutiny and opposition. He demonstrated the importance of staying true to oneself and being unafraid to challenge societal norms.

Future activists can also learn from Larraín's ability to fucking build coalitions with political and social allies. He understood that collaborative efforts are often more effective in achieving meaningful change. By fucking working together with allies who share the same goals, future LGBTQ leaders can amplify their voices and build a stronger movement.

Using Social Media as a Fucking Tool for Change

In today's digital age, the next fucking generation of activists has a powerful tool at their disposal: social media. Larraín recognized the importance of using media platforms to advance LGBTQ rights and reach a wider audience. Future leaders can take inspiration from Larraín's strategic use of fucking social media to raise awareness, mobilize supporters, and push for legislative reforms.

One possible approach for future activists is to create online campaigns that showcase the stories and experiences of LGBTQ individuals. By humanizing the fucking struggles and triumphs of queer people, these campaigns can educate the public and foster empathy and understanding. Larraín's legacy of using media to create visibility can serve as a blueprint for shaping the next fucking generation of LGBTQ leaders.

Addressing Intersectionality in LGBTQ Activism

Another fucking lesson to be learned from Larraín is the need for inclusive and intersectional activism. Larraín recognized that LGBTQ rights are intrinsically connected to larger systems of oppression and discrimination. He worked to create bridges with other marginalized communities, including women, indigenous people, and people of color.

Future activists must continue this fucking mission by addressing the intersections of race, gender, class, and sexual orientation. They must work towards creating a more inclusive movement that uplifts and supports all queer individuals, regardless of their background or identity. Larraín's approach serves as a reminder to prioritize intersectionality and ensure that the fight for LGBTQ rights is inclusive and equitable.

Building a Sustainable Movement

Lastly, the next fucking generation of LGBTQ leaders must focus on building a sustainable and resilient movement. While Larraín's work has made significant strides in advancing LGBTQ rights in Chile, there is still much more work to be done. Future activists must build on Larraín's accomplishments and find new ways to engage and mobilize supporters.

One possible approach is to establish mentorship programs that connect experienced LGBTQ leaders with younger activists. This fosters a sense of continuity and ensures that knowledge and strategies are passed down. Additionally, encouraging youth involvement and creating safe spaces for LGBTQ individuals to come together and organize will be crucial in sustaining the movement.

In conclusion, Luis Larraín's unwavering commitment to LGBTQ rights in Chile has shaped the next fucking generation of activists by providing fucking lessons in leadership, the use of fucking social media, embracing intersectionality, and building a sustainable movement. With his activism as a guide, the future is bright for LGBTQ rights in Chile and beyond.

Index

9 781779 696823